A ROPE—IN CASE

When Lillian Beckwith first came to Bruach, in the
Hebrides, she was told: 'Always carry a rope—in case'.
And whether it was for repairing a fence, tying up a
boat or securing the roof of the local taxi, there was no
denying the wisdom of the advice.

The fourth of Lillian Beckwith's books about her life
on Bruach, A ROPE—IN CASE, is packed with the hi-
larious incidents and delightful characters that readers
of THE HILLS IS LONELY, THE SEA FOR BREAK-
FAST and THE LOUD HALO have enjoyed so much.

Also in Arrow Books by Lillian Beckwith

Lillian Beckwith

A ROPE–IN CASE

Decorations
by
DOUGLAS HALL

ARROW BOOKS

Arrow Books Limited
3 Fitzroy Square, London W1

An imprint of the Hutchinson Publishing Group

London Melbourne Sydney Auckland
Wellington Johannesburg and agencies
throughout the world

First published by
Hutchinson & Co (Publishers) Ltd 1968
Second impression 1969
Arrow edition October 1970
Second impression November 1970
Third impression September 1971
Fourth impression June 1972
Fifth impression July 1973
Sixth impression June 1974
Seventh impression April 1975
Eighth impression April 1977

Made and printed in Great Britain
by The Anchor Press Ltd
Tiptree, Essex

ISBN 0 09 906640 8

For Ted

Contents

Vocabulary

		(Approximate pronunciation)
Cailleach	Old Woman	Kyle-yak
Mo ghaoil	My dear	Mo gale
Ceilidh	An impromptu meeting	Cayley
Strupak	A cup of tea and a bite to eat	Stroopak
Oidhche mhath!	Goodnight	Oi-she-va
Cnoc	Knoll	Crock
Sithean	A Fairy Dwelling	Sheehan
Ciamar a Tha	'How are you?'	Camera How?

A Rope—In Case

THE March morning was full of mist; grey and inscrutable the swirling formations loped in from the sea to hover uncertainly over the village of Bruach so that the houses and crofts vanished and re-emerged in a constantly changing pattern; the land appeared to be adrift in a thick silence through which the distant throbbing of the burn and the nearer rasp of tide on shingle barely, penetrated. 'For every day of mist in March there'll be an inch of snow in May,' the old crofters predicted. This was our fourth day of mist in the first fourteen days of March so it looked as if we must expect an exceedingly cold May.

I had finished breakfast, milked my cow and fed the poultry and now I was preparing to catch the bus which would take me on the first stage of my visit to the mainland. The preparations entailed no searching of a wardrobe and debating which garments I should wear. A trip to the mainland meant an early morning start and an evening return and as the weather could change dramatically in that time it was necessary always to play safe and wear one's toughest shoes, well polished for the occasion, and one's most dependable waterproof which would have a sou-wester tucked into a pocket. I dropped my shoes into the shopping bag I was taking and pulled on a pair of thick socks and gumboots over my stockings. The path was wet and muddy so I would change into shoes when I reached the bus and leave the socks and gumboots under a seat ready for my return. Giving the fire a final damping down with wet peats and dross I reached up and took my waterproof from the hook beside the door and with it a length of rope which hung on an adjoining hook. It was instinct now to open the door cautiously so as not to disturb any wild life that might have ventured near in the early silence. I was so often rewarded for my caution; perhaps with the sight of a buzzard surveying the world from the top of the clothes line post; perhaps it would be a rabbit drinking from the hens' water bowl or a seal close inshore eyeing the cottages as if he would like to be invited in for breakfast. But then again it might only be a hooded crow loitering with such intent over my chicken run that I had to clap my hands to drive him away. This morning the

mist hid any secret there might have been and I pulled the
door shut behind me. It was unthinkable to lock a door in
Bruach even when one was leaving the house for a whole day.
Outside I paused, looking at the length of rope I still held in
my hand. Foolish of me, I thought, it wasn't necessary to
take a rope with me on what after all was to be in the nature
of a day off from work. For a moment I hesitated wondering
whether I should go back and replace the rope on its hook
but with a shrug I dropped it into the bag along with my
shoes. It seemed less trouble to take it.

When I had first come to the Hebrides Morag, my land-
lady had advised me always to 'take a rope—in case', and
when I moved into my own cottage a length of rope hung
on the hook next to my outdoor clothes so that it was a
habit to reach for a coat in one hand and the rope in the
other. In fact it had become such an essential adjunct that
I felt bereft if I was not carrying it somewhere about my
person. Over and over again I had proved its usefulness. I
might need it to catch a calf or a sheep; to carry a bundle
of hay to the cow or a can of paraffin from the grocer; to
tie a bundle of driftwood I had collected, or a sack of peat;
to secure a boat; make a temporary repair to a sagging fence
or a halter for a horse. In stormy weather there was nothing
so good as a rope tied round the waist for preventing one's
clothes from billowing up above one's head. Excepting when
they were going on holiday or to church the Bruach crofters
were rarely without a length of rope, either coiled around an
arm or protruding from a pocket.

The bus driver blew a blast on his horn as I came out of
the mist and I suspected that either I was late or he was in
a bad temper.

'I'm sorry,' I began, 'Am I late?'

'No, I don't think so.' His voice was affable. 'It's just that

I want to see to a couple of my snares on the way so I thought I'd just hurry folks up a bit so I could get started.

Such unscheduled changes caused no complaint in Bruach and the driver was equally willing to similarly oblige his passengers.

I sat down beside Janet. 'You have a good poc,' she commented, noticing my capacious shopping bag. Janet always managed to make her observations with a sort of disparaging admiration so that I felt I had to excuse the size of my bag by telling her I was expecting to bring home a fair number of purchases.

'You're not wantin' to catch the train, then?' she asked. 'No,' I told her.

'I'm thinkin' it's just as well,' she comforted. 'For the dear knows how long it will take him to see to his snares.'

'Ach, that man an' his snares,' interposed Erchy, who was sitting behind us. 'He forgets he's here for drivin' the bus when he's after the rabbits.'

It took the driver no more than a quarter of an hour to attend to his snares and when he returned he dumped three dead rabbits on top of the pile of mailbags. In three of the private mail-boxes where he stopped to collect letters he left a rabbit in exchange.

'What's the time?' he asked, resuming his seat after the last mail-box had been emptied. No-one replied. My watch had not functioned for months and yet I had hardly been inconvenienced by the lack of it. Time was so rarely referred to in Bruach. The bus driver repeated the question in Gaelic, shouting at old Farquhar who was very deaf. Ponderously the old man took out his cherished watch and showed him. 'We'd best get a move on,' the driver warned. The mist still enveloped us but on the Bruach road one could be fairly certain of meeting no other traffic so early in the morning. He put his foot well down on the accelerator.

'Oh, how I hate the mist!' said Janet feelingly. There were murmurs of almost passionate assent from the rest of the passengers. Bruachites, especially the women, did indeed dislike the mist. It seemed to emphasize the loneliness and isolation of their lives, cutting them off from the reassuring view of other cottages where they knew company was their's for the seeking.

The road twisted and climbed around the steep shores of the loch. As we climbed higher the mist thinned so that soon we were looking down on curling banks of it as one looks down on to cloud from an aeroplane.

'There's a wind on the wireless,' the driver called over his shoulder and at once everyone became more cheerful. Wind would soon drive the mist away.

The mainland village was squalid and colourless. This may have been because it was within a day's journey of a large town, or perhaps because it was too long since its inhabitants had forsaken the crofting life in favour of commerce. Whatever the reason I found it a cold and cheerless place to spend a day. It was only when there was a compelling need for some tool or material, the lack of which was holding up a long extended task, that it became in any way endurable for me.

'Have you much shoppin' to do?' enquired Janet when we had disembarked from the island ferry.

'Yes, quite a bit, I want some felt and roofing nails for the poultry shed. And some vegetables if I can get them.' I scanned my list. 'Oh, and Sarah's asked me to try to get her a "man-chine for the calf's nose",' I added with a smile. Janet smiled too. To Sarah most things contrived by man were 'man-chines'. Cars and lorries were acceptably enough 'man-chines' but it was more difficult to interpret her description of a broom as a 'man-chine for cleaning floors' and a pillar-box as a 'man-chine for posting letters'. The 'man-chine' she had asked me to get for her now was merely a U-shaped flap of wood which fitted into the calf's nostrils and prevented it from sucking the cow while still allowing it to graze adequately.

'You'd think Yawn could make her one,' said Janet.

'Yawn says he's made her dozens and that she's lost the lot. He thinks if she has to pay for one out of her own money she'll take better care of it.'

'I doubt she will,' said Janet.

There were no more than a half dozen shops in the village, one of which was a tearoom. There was also a small hotel. We visited first a poky general store where they sold meat and bacon, bread and groceries and shoes and drapery all from one littered counter. The varied smells that assailed us were dominated by the odour of old cabbages and softening onions in rolled-down sacks on the floor. Janet was trying on a pair of shoes when old Farquhar came in and announced that he wanted 'two bread loafs an' a pound of wee beefies.' Dourly the assistant handed him two large loaves and then proceeded to weigh out a pound of mince.

'What a glamorous name for mince,' I murmured to Janet. 'It makes it sound quite appetising.' When my turn came I too asked for a pound of 'wee beefies'. The assistant flicked me a look of disdain.

'Is it mince you're after wantin'?' he asked severely.

I went with Janet to the chemist where she bought half a stone of baking soda to alleviate the indigestion which afflicted all her family and then she came with me to the chandler's to order my roofing felt and nails. While the assistant was counting out the nails for me old Farquhar came shuffling in.

'Haff you any sea boots?' he demanded.

'Aye, we have plenty,' was the crisp reply. Old Farquhar leaned forward, his hand cupped to his ear.

'All that lot there,' shouted the man, indicating the line of boots in all sizes that stretched across the back of the shop.

Farquhar gave them a cursory glance. 'Thank you very much, I will take two,' he said with lofty indifference.

We had finished our shopping within the hour and as it was too wet to go for a walk and too early to get lunch we went into the tea room where we drank tea and chatted with the waitress who turned out to be a relative of Janet's. Following that we ambled up to the hotel, locally known as 'Kipper Hall' and ate kippers and turnips and potatoes and declined a pool of rice pudding. Janet, by discreet questioning, discovered that the hotel cook was also a relative of hers and sent the waitress to convey the discovery to her which resulted in an invitation to take tea in the kitchen. We were seated cosily in front of the fire exchanging news and gossip when the door was pushed open and Erchy appeared. He was carrying a large tin of foot-rot ointment.

'Ah, they told me I would find you here,' he greeted us.

'Come away in,' invited the cook and poured out another cup of tea.

Erchy came in and sat down.

'Are you wantin' us, then?' Janet asked.

'I was wantin' Miss Peckwitt,' he admitted.

I glanced at him in surprise. 'Why me?' I asked.

'Well, you mind I came out to see would I get a look at a boat I was thinkin' of buyin'?' Janet and I nodded. 'Aye, well it seems she's out in a place a few miles from here an' I cannot get a car to take me there.'

'Too far to walk?' I asked.

'Aye, in the time I have before the bus goes away again an' I'm no so keen to stay the night here.'

'So why were you looking for me?' I asked.

'It's this way,' he began, and went on to tell me that there was a car available but there was no driver. The old man who owned the car had been banned from driving but if I would agree to drive it he would be very pleased to let us have the car for as long as we wished.

'Okay,' I agreed. 'So long as we're back in time for the bus.'

Janet decided to come with us 'just for the drive' and we collected the car from an extremely co-operative garage proprietor. The mist had by now been harried away to the hills by a bullying wind that was ushering thick spongy looking clouds in its place. Before we had gone more than half a mile they had wrung themselves out and the windscreen wipers worked steadily.

'I met a relative of yours when I went for a drink,' Erchy told Janet.

'Another?' I laughed. 'She's already discovered two this morning.'

'Aye, well this fellow's newly back from America. He's been out there near enough to twenty-five years.'

Janet was agog with interest. 'It wouldn't be yon Uisdean who married my cousin's cousin from Uist?' She and Erchy delved into genealogies.

'That was him then that went away because of the ghost,' she told us when identification was completed satisfactorily. 'I didn't think he'd ever come back to these parts.'

'Is it him?' Erchy accepted her statement without surprise. 'Aye well he hasn't lost his taste for whisky while he's been away.'

'Ach, no,' Janet assured him. 'He would still draw the same breath.'

'What ghost is this you're talking about?' I asked.

'You mind the one. You must have heard of it.' Janet was emphatic.

'I don't think I have,' I said.

'Well, this fellow, this sort of cousin of mine was walkin' home one night when he met a strange woman He greeted her with a "Ciamar a Tha" just the same as he would any-one but as soon as he's spoken this woman turns and walks alongside him and tells him that he's the first person to have spoken to her for many years. He knew fine she was a ghost then an' tried to hurry away but she would follow him. She told him she had not died by her own hand as people thought but that she had been murdered. She named her killer and pleaded with the man to go to the authorities and have the murderer brought to justice. He had to say he would, just to get rid of her but he didn't do any more about it. The next time he was that way she pursued him again, pleadin' an' pleadin'. He still didn't do anythin' about it but she upset him so much he packed up an' went to America.'

'I've never heard that story before,' I told her.

'Indeed?' Janet's voice was puzzled. 'It's well known in these parts.' The three of us became deep in thought for a few minutes and then Janet spoke again. 'I wonder if it's just a lot of nonsense?'

'What, the story or the ghost?' I asked.

'No, indeed.' Janet sounded prickly. 'The man wouldn't have told a lie. No, I was thinkin' about the belief we have hereabouts that a ghost can't cross water. That's why he went to America, you see. But I'd like to know if it's true or not. It's a pity Erchy didn't know who it was an' then he could have asked him.'

Erchy said, 'Aye, well it's too late now. He was catchin'

the train back to Glasgow an' he's away back on his travels by the weekend.'

We drove on in silence. 'What a nice man that garage proprietor seems to be,' I said.

'Aye,' Erchy admitted shortly.

'He didn't seem to be able to do enough for us,' added Janet.

'Aye.'

It was unlike Erchy to be so terse but Janet and I knew that questions would bring no information. We waited patiently.

'You mind that net I sold about three years back?' Erchy asked Janet at last.

'I mind that fine. It wasn't a net just, was it?'

'No, but the net was the chief thing.'

'I remember that,' she said.

'Well, it was to that very man I sold them. He didn't have the money to pay for them then but he said he'd see me right so I let him have them. I've never seen a penny from him since.'

'The man!' ejaculated Janet.

'He looks to be doing well enough now,' I remarked. The garage had been flanked by a shop bearing the same name and both had looked highly prosperous.

'He's doin' fine,' Erchy corroborated. 'He was tellin' me himself of all the trouble he has with the Income Tax. He says they're always after him.'

'He must be doin' well if he has the Income Tax after him,' said Janet, knowledgeably.

'Aye, he was tellin' me he had a letter from them wantin' money round about Christmas time so he sent them a Christmas card with his reply. He wrote on it "A Merry

Christmas to you ye buggers" and he repeated "ye buggers" wherever there was space all over the card.'

'That was no very nice of him,' Janet observed.

'He was pleased enough with it,' said Erchy. 'He believes he fairly spoiled their Christmas for them.'

'An all this time he's never paid you for your net,' Janet was indignant.

'No, he has not.'

'Have you asked him for the money?' That was my question. Janet, being a Gael would never have suggested such a thing could happen.

'Indeed no!' Erchy was shocked.

'Maybe it's just as well you took his car, then,' Janet told him. 'You'll maybe get a bit of somethin' back from it.'

'It's a shame we don't have the time to go for a good drive round on his petrol while we have the chance,' he said. 'There's plenty in the tank.'

'We could have fairly enjoyed ourselves,' Janet said regretfully.

Erchy inspected the boat he had been thinking of buying, rejected it with the pronouncement that it would 'float like a bundle of hay' and was ready to return. Back at the garage the beaming proprietor greeted us effusively. Erchy's hand wavered in the region of his breast pocket subtly indicating that he had money to pay if the man should have the cheek to ask for it. Just as subtly the other conveyed that no mention of money must be made.

'Take the car any time you're wantin' it,' he told Erchy and seemed affronted that we had used so little petrol. I got the feeling that had we damaged the car he would have welcomed the opportunity to display further magnanimity. He was insistent that we took tea with him and his wife and led us into a passage which went from the garage to a newly built extension of the old croft house. Here we sat on modern chairs and were urged to eat quantities of shop biscuits while the old woman poured out cup after cup of thick black tea that looked as if we should need knives and forks to wrestle with it.

It was time to go. We shook hands all round and thanked them for their hospitality, assuring them of reciprocal cordiality if they should ever come to Bruach. Only Erchy seemed to be a little 'tongue in cheek' with his remarks.

At the pier we found the tide was out and picked our way to the ferry over slippery weed while spray splashed and shed itself over us. Just as the ferry was about to leave there came a shout and we perceived the garage proprietor running down to the jetty, gesticulating and shouting Erchy's name. Erchy went forward to meet him.

'I was thinkin' I'd never catch you,' panted the man, as he handed Erchy a parcel. 'You left this behind you in the car an' I didn't notice it until this minute just.'

Erchy gave a nod of pleased recollection. 'Aye, that's right so I did,' he said, taking the parcel. 'I don't know what I'd do without it.'

He rejoined Janet and me. 'Erchy, I'm sure there was no parcel left in that car,' I told him. Janet and I were most careful to check.'

Erchy gave me an enigmatic smile. 'Damty sure there wasn't,' he agreed. He opened the parcel and revealed a carton of five hundred cigarettes. They were of a brand I knew he never smoked and to my look of astonishment he explained: 'This is just the man's way of payin' me for my net. Now we're both satisfied.'

It was so cold and wet on the ferry that the man who should have collected our fares chose not to leave the shelter of the wheelhouse, allowing us to make the journey free.

'He's no seein' us,' murmured Janet, in the Bruach idiom.

'Not like it is in the summer,' Erchy commented. 'Then, when there's plenty tourists on the ferry they won't take it near the pier till they've got all the fares. They just keep circlin' round makin' sure no-one can walk off without payin first.'

On the island quay stood an aged and dispirited touring car with most of its side windows missing. The bus driver waited beside it.

'The buss is broken,' he announced. His tone made the disaster sound an everyday occurrence.

'Broken?' Janet exclaimed.

'Aye. It's away to the garage an' they're sayin' they'll not likely get it sorted before midnight.' There was a trace of exultant pessimism about him.

'So we've got to get home in this thing.' I said, peering into the car's unkempt interior.

'Unless you'll stay for the dance,' the driver proposed eagerly. 'There's to be a good dance on here tonight an' I wouldn't mind stayin' for it.'

'Oh, my,' said Janet, already half persuaded. For her a dance promised a bevy of friends and a good ceilidh in some crowded corner of the room.

Erchy said thoughtfully, 'I've a mind to stay myself.'

They all looked at me. 'I must get home,' I protested. 'I've got a cow and hens to see to tonight yet.'

'Ach, I can get a message for someone to see to your beasts for you,' the driver assured me.

'No need,' I insisted heartlessly. 'If there's a car to take me. I'm going back now.'

'There's a car all right but you've not heard yet who's goin' to drive it.' The driver smiled wickedly and mentioned a name. 'An' he has a good drink on him already,' he added.

with relish. I felt myself go pale. The Bruach road ran steeply along the side of the loch and at times there were literally only inches separating the wheels of the bus from the crumbling edge of the road. With a shudder I recollected the one hair-raising journey I had endured with the driver he mentioned. For weeks afterwards in my dreams I repeatedly found myself in pieces at the bottom of some precipice.

'I'm not going with him,' I said flatly.

'Then stay for the dance,' the driver wheedled.

'No.' I knew I was being cruel but it was his job to drive the bus and I badly wanted to get home.

'Ach, you'd enjoy yourself,' he persisted.

'I would not,' I told him. 'I don't know a soul here. Nobody would ask me to dance.'

'There's Erchy. He'll dance with you.'

'Erchy will do all his dancing in the bar,' I said.

'I'll give you a dance myself.' His tone was generous.

'Thankyou,' I countered. 'And what would I do the rest of the time? Just sit there looking out of things and not knowing what to do with myself, I suppose.'

'Ach, Miss Peckwitt, there's no need for that. Just you eat a couple of them figs you can buy from the grocer. When you're not dancin' it gives you somethin' to do pickin' all the seeds out of your teeths. It's what I do myself when I'm at a dance in a strange place.'

Janet turned on him. 'That's all right for you,' she told him, 'but Miss Peckwitt has her own teeth. They're not false ones like yours.'

'Oh,' said the driver, a little taken aback. 'That might not be so good then.'

He suggested that we should go for a cup of tea while he made arrangements for the car and another driver. Half an hour later he was back and commanding us to get into the car.

'Are you no stayin' for the dance, then?' Janet asked. He muttered petulantly.

The only vacant places were beside old Farquhar who was ensconced majestically in the middle of the back seat. We were about to climb in beside him when the driver stopped us.

'No, you cannot go in there. You'll just have to squeeze up with the others,' he instructed us. 'There's a ram I'm to pick up in a wee whiley an' he'll need to go in the back seat.' He requested the passengers to lift up their feet and dumped my roll of felt on the floor.

It took four men to get the struggling ram into the back of the car, where full mail bags were strategically placed so as to restrict its movement. Even so Farquhar had to crouch with the animal between his legs while he held on to its horns. The rest of us huddled together with our knees bumping our chins as the old car bounced from pothole to pothole and we tried not to take too much notice of the strugglings and gruntings that came from the seat behind us along with the overpowering smell of wet fleece.

The wind was rising rapidly to a gale; the sea came foaming in beneath a mist of spray. Every now and then the driver looked up at the hood which was lifting and banging ominously. 'You'd best some of you hang on to that,' he advised and those who were nearest grabbed whatever hand-hold they could. We reached the head of the loch where the wind funnelled in from the sea and rushed screaming through the narrow strath between two ranges of hills. There was a shout of alarm as a sudden gust, stronger than any before it, thrust at the car, threatening to overturn it. We all ducked as the driver grappled with the wheel. The moment over, we

sat up and saw in the same instant that there was no longer
a hood on the car. Twisting round in our seats we could see
the heavy canvas trailing like a broken kite behind. The
driver stopped and all the passengers except Farquhar who
was wrestling with an increasingly panic-stricken ram
tumbled out to capture the hood. We fought the wind as we
tried to pull it back over the car and secure it but the
fasteners had gone and we had to stand holding it, awaiting
instructions from the driver.

'Wait now till I get a rope!' he shouted and rooted under
his seat. He produced a length of rope and passed one end
under the car to a helper on the other side who pulled it up.
With the wind tearing at their clothes they scrambled together
trying to tie it over the hood. The driver swore. 'The damty
thing's not long enough.' Turning to us he asked: 'Anybody
got a piece of rope?'

'I have,' I replied. 'Hold on to this while I get it.' He
weighed down on the section of hood I had been holding
while I retrieved the piece of rope from the bottom of my
shopping bag.

'That'll do it,' he said, snatching it from me. He tied the
two ropes together and we surveyed the repair briefly before
climbing back into our seats.

'I only brought that rope in case the old car needed a tow,'
the driver said.

I murmured to Janet that there would be little hope of
getting a tow on the deserted Bruach road. She looked
slightly puzzled.

'We're not likely to meet a car to give us a tow,' I pointed
out.

'Oh, no, mo ghaoil. He wouldn't be thinkin' of a motor
to pull us.' She glanced round. 'There are plenty of us here.'

We reached Bruach without further mishap and juddered

to a stop outside the Post Office. 'What's wrong with the old car?' demanded the postman, coming out to collect the mailbags. 'She looks as if she's got the toothache or somethin'.'

'I doubt she would have lost her top if it hadn't been for Miss Peckwitt here havin' a wee bitty rope with her,' the driver told him.

I permitted myself a smug smile. 'Oh, I always take a rope in case,' I said.

A Change in the Weather

EVEN by Hebridean standards the weather during the month of May was atrocious. 'Severe gale force nine' and 'storm force ten' were predicted, realised and endured. Communal potato planting was accomplished on the few days when there was a brief respite from the stinging rain and hail, when we had to contend only with 'gale force eight' winds that tore at the long winter mane of the young plough horse and threatened to wrest the hair from the head of any woman who did not attend constantly to the tightening of the knot of her headscarf. The men pulled on their caps back to front and jammed them well down over their foreheads as was their habit in wild weather. We all wore at least one pair of thick woolly socks inside our gumboots and we all had ropes tied round our waists to discourage our coats from flying above our heads as we bent to the task of planting. The women complained of the cold wind blowing up their skirts and were outspoken in envying the men their long woollen underpants. They congratulated me on my wisdom in wearing slacks and though I smiled in polite acknowledgment I knew perfectly well that they would sooner freeze to death than outrage the biblical traditionalism of their own attire.

The wind, like a heavy hand in the small of our backs, pushed us along as we hurried to and fro with our pails of potatoes and fertiliser. It filled our mouths, whipping away the instructions we shouted to one another so that we had to resort to mime. It made futile the directions Erchy, the ploughman, shouted to his horse so that he had to resort to vituperation. Man and animal grew increasingly exasperated at the lack of co-ordination in their efforts. Dung flew about us as the men carried it forkful by forkful from the scattered heaps to the furrows while one or two of the older, hardier women, unable to endure seeing good dung wasted, scraped it up in their bare hands and placed it, almost lovingly, in the rows. Those of us who, like myself, were responsible for seeing that each potato was given a generous helping of 'guano' (in Bruach all artificial manures were referred to as 'guano') were ourselves liberally coated with the dusty grey

chemical. It smarted on our wind-burned lips and cheeks
and made our eyes run with tears.

'Oh, my, but it's coarse, coarse, coarse,' we complained
to one another as we mustered in the croft house for a
welcome mid-morning strupak.

'Indeed but I'm after havin' a job to keep the plough in
the ground with the strength of it,' grumbled Erchy. He gave
three loud belches in quick succession. 'Every time I open
my mouth to shout at the horse the wind rushes in and fills
my stomach,' he excused himself. He pushed back his cap,
exposing the broad weal that marked the boundary between
his wind-crimsoned face and the sheltered area above.

I became aware that Hamish, the owner of the croft we
were planting, was beckoning me towards the door.

'I'm thinkin' of changin' Sarah to plantin' potatoes,' he
confided. 'She's no good with the guano.'

I looked at him questioningly. Sarah admitted to being
seventy-nine years of age and to me she had appeared to be
working as well as anyone else at spreading the guano.

'Ach, her back's too stiff and she canna bend it right,'
Hamish said.

'Surely she'll have to bend even lower if she has to plant
the potatoes?' I pointed out.

'No, that's not the way of it at all,' he argued. 'She can
drop the potatoes in the furrows easy enough and they'll land
somewhere abouts even if it's no the right place. It's kind of
different with the guano. When she drops a handful of it in
this wind then it's away before it gets to the furrow. The
potatoes will be missin' it, likely.'

'Is it the potatoes is missin' it?' expostulated Angus, who
had been listening to our conversation. 'Man, I'm thinkin'
it's not just your potatoes but your whole damty croft that's
missin' it.'

At last everyone's potatoes were planted and we were able to return to our neglected chores while the rain renewed its onslaught. In Bruach, rain after ploughing was always welcome. It smoothed the ridged furrows and washed the earth into the gaps left by the often inexpert ploughing. We could sit back and think with deep satisfaction of the rich solution of dung and guano in which our potatoes would already be steeping.

As May drew to a close the weather grew even less spring like. Hailstones frequently racketed against the windows and the iron roofs of our cottages and barns, and the snow which, during a warm spell in April, had disappeared from all but the peaks of the hills now spread downwards again to clothe them with white capuchons. Some of us began to wonder if the warm spell had been the only good weather we should get that year but then, on the evening of the last day of the month, the baleful clouds which had shrouded us for so long parted their skirts to reveal the promising afterglow of a sunset that tinged the snow with apricot and edged the western horizon with gold. The wind gave way to noisy gusts, fierce but sporadic, the stillness between them softened by a perceptible warmth. Even before I retired for the night the sky was clear except for a few clouds thin as foam that drifted serenely. Moon shadows spread from the rowan tree and the old barn and only the noise of the swell banging pettishly against the rocks of the shore reminded me of the savagery there had been.

On the first morning of June I washed up my breakfast dishes and sang as I worked to the accompaniment of varying creaks from the corrugated iron roof of the lean-to kitchen as it shrugged and settled itself in response to a calm, rejoicing sun. It was always good to hear those creaks; to know that once again there was real warmth in the air and that, for a few hours at least, plans could be made to carry out work that could only be done satisfactorily in calm, dry weather.

I was putting out the sodden doormats to dry on the stone dyke when Morag arrived. She was wearing a thick navy sweater that proclaimed her to be a member of a well known steamship company; over her skirt she wore a clean sack apron and on her head was tied a square of white cloth liberally stained with brown. It looked suspiciously like the cloth she used for boiling the large fruit dumplings she made when she was expecting a visit from the missionary or someone equally impressive.

'There's a right change in the weather,' she greeted me. 'An' amn't I glad to see the back of all that rain.'

I agreed heartily and indicated the row of footwear along the wall of the cottage, tilted towards the sun.

'I haven't a dry pair of boots or shoes to my name,' I complained. Soggy gumboots are not only cold and miserable for the feet, they are exceedingly difficult to pull on, and throughout my stay in the Hebrides my conception of Heaven was a never-ending supply of dry socks and dry gumboots.

'It's the same with myself, just,' Morag admitted. 'Here's me with hay in my tackety boots at this very minute to see will I keep my feet dry.' Most of us stuffed hay into our wet boots when we took them off but we emptied it out before we wore them again.

'It sounds a bit uncomfortable,' I said.

'Not at all,' she denied. 'An' it's keepin' my feets nice an' warm.'

Together we assessed the portent of the gentle blue of the sky and the few frayed clouds caught on the hill peaks. Down on the rocks slow breakers were still coming in rearing and breaking but out at sea only fitful white wave crests glinted in the sunlight.

'If we would get a day or so of this we'd be able to have the lorry bring home our peats, likely,' Morag suggested.

'It'll take more than a couple of days to dry out the moors enough for a lorry to get to my peats,' I retorted. Due to my being a latecomer to peat cutting my peat hag was, naturally, the most inaccessible of all.

'Ach, so long as there's a good skin on the ground the lorry would get, I doubt,' insisted Morag blandly.

'I doubt you said that last year,' I taxed her. 'And remember how the lorry got bogged time after time and what hard work it was digging it out? Remember how the driver swore he'd never take any notice of you again?' I continued relentlessly. Morag looked a little discomfited. 'I'm not going to risk being made a fool of again this year,' I added meaningly.

'Oh, but, mo ghaoil, nobody made a fool of you,' Morag hastened to reassure me. 'It was just the way things turned out.'

'Oh, of course,' I agreed.

The previous year several of us had clubbed together to hire a lorry to transport our stacks of peats home, the idea being that we all helped one another to load and unload, sharing equally the cost of the hire. On the face of it the scheme may have looked unfair to those who, like myself, had cut a relatively small number of peats whereas the larger families prided themselves on having a dozen stacks or more but as the larger the family the more helpers they provided the arrangement worked to everyone's satisfaction.

The lorry had arrived in charge of Willy Ruag ('Red Willy'), it's exuberant driver but even Willy scratched at his tawny head and muttered dubiously when he saw how far from the track some of the peat stacks were situated. However, in response to Morag's assuring him airily that

there was 'skin enough on the moors to take a steam roller',
he yielded so far as to take the lorry alongside the stacks
nearest the road.

It had been a glorious day for work. The sun shone
uninhibitedly but it was accompanied by a breeze that was
enough to keep us cool and save us from the attentions of
the vicious clegs (horseflies), yet not capricious enough to
subject us to the torment of having our eyes continuously
filled with peat dust. We all, including the ever-obliging
Willy, set to work throwing the peats up into the lorry. There
was no pattern to our throwing; everyone pitched peats with
haphazard enthusiasm from all directions amid a constant
flow of lighthearted banter with only an occasional shout of
laughing recrimination to betray the fact that a peat had hit
one of the loaders on the other side of the lorry. When the
load had grown precariously high the driver called a halt
and climbed up into the cab. We all stood back, rubbing
peat dust from our reddening arms and faces. With a shudder
the lorry started and simultaneously there came a snarling
grumble from the rear wheels as they broke through the
dried crust of the moor and spun themselves into the bog-
giness beneath. The distressed face of the driver peered out
of the cab. The non-mechanically minded Bruachites, seemingly unaware of the likely consequence, exhorted him to
carry on. Obediently Willy tried again but the wheels only
spun themselves deeper into the soft ground. He called us to
push and we all flung ourselves at the lorry with boisterous
determination, even old Sarah lending her thin aged arms
to the task. After half an hour of strenuous pushing and
devising the anxiety I felt had begun to affect the Bruachites,
though there were still eruptions of laughter above the
murmured comments. When, inevitably, the order came to
unload they greeted it without chagrin. For them the

dilemma was an event; one that would have its place in the retailed anecdotes of the village and to which other more mundane happenings could be related in time. 'I mind she calved the day before yon lorry that was loadin' peats got stuck in the bog. . . .'

When the unloading was almost finished and the remaining peats had been piled at the rear of the chassis Willy tried again to coax the lorry forward but by this time the ruts were deeper and squelchier. Erchy was dispatched to bring sacks from the village while the rest of us were commanded to go and gather stones from the bed of the burn and eventually with these aids and renewed efforts by the loaders the lorry was at last clear of the bog. Willy's worried face peering from the cab broke into a relieved grin. We cheered as the lorry juddered forward. We ceased to cheer as Willy drove on and we realised he was not going to stop again until he had reached the firm ground of the track and that we should now have to carry all the peats over to the lorry before throwing them up. I was already wilting with dismay but the Bruachites, inured as they were to constant frustrations, accepted the extra work with patient good humour. So long as they worked in company their spirits were never dampened for long and soon the smiles were back and the joking had begun again.

'Did anybody feed your hens for you yet?' Morag asked me just before it was the turn of my peats to be loaded.

'Goodness, no,' I admitted ruefully, not having noticed until she spoke how near to the hill peaks the sun had travelled. Spring days in the Hebrides are long and night began nominally when the sun disappeared behind the first of the peaks. The poultry too seemed to accept this as a sign of the end of their day and if I did not attend to them in time they would go sulkily to roost without their evening feed. Experience had taught me that sulkiness and hunger had a disastrous effect on egg-laying.

'You'd best go back with Willy on this load and then see an' catch him again on the way back,' Morag advised.

I climbed into the cab beside Willy Ruag, asking him to drop me off at my croft and to look out for me on his way back. Willy nodded acceptance of the arrangement. As I had expected my hens were grouped querulously around the door of the cottage and when they caught sight of my approach they ran towards me, their feet stamping noisily on the dry ground. They crowded about me, pecking at my feet and impeding my progress until there came several indignant screeches accompanied by much wing flapping as I inadvertantly trod on some of them. They were accustomed to having a good bowl of mash at night for which they were in the habit of queueing at least an hour before it was ready. Tonight, however, there was no time for mash-making so I filled their bowl with corn—a repeat of their morning feed—and hoped they would be deluded. Keeping an ear alert for the sound of the returning lorry I brewed myself a quick cup of coffee and hastily munched a slice of home-made bread spread thickly with home-made butter and crowdie. Between sips and bites I raced to collect the day's eggs from the nest-boxes; took in the sun-warmed washing, which had already been out for two nights, and then gratefully flopped down on the wooden bench outside, reflecting as I watched the sunset burning the sky behind the dark positive peaks of the hills how lucky I was to be living in such surroundings.

Half an hour later I was no longer reflective. There had been plenty of time for the lorry to be unloaded but there was still no sign of its return. Had Willy stopped for a prolonged strupak? Surely not, I argued. After a long day and with everyone waiting for him to resume loading he would

undoubtedly be in a hurry to get finished. I waited for another
quarter of an hour and then thinking that in some inexplicable way I had missed seeing or hearing the lorry I got up,
stretched my reluctant limbs and started to walk.

It was a rough plod of nearly two miles to the peat moors
but it was a plod made so frequently either to work at peats
or to milk, feed or inspect cattle that with time it had become
for me no more demanding than a short walk to the shops
would have been when I lived in town. Small children
walked twice the distance to school and back each day and
were not considered hard done by. Old men, who spurned
the idea of a 'wee hoosie', did not consider there was privacy
enough for them to relieve their bowels unless there was a
good two miles of moor between themselves and their homes.
(They suffered a good deal from constipation during spells
of very bad weather.) The women thought nothing of making
the trudge two or three times a day between household
chores. As an instance of this I recall during my early days in
Bruach calling at the house of one of my neighbours who had
very kindly offered to allow me to cut peats from one of her
own hags until I should find someone to 'skin' my own. She
had promised to come with me to show me which particular
hag this was, since the moors were scarred all over with hags
and, to the uninitiated, one was no different from another.
When I arrived at her house, carrying my peat iron and all
ready for work, I found her entertaining a party of friends
from a neighbouring village. I made my apologies and was
about to withdraw when my neighbour put down her cup
of tea, threw a cardigan over her shoulders and announced
that she was ready to accompany me.

'But you mustn't leave your friends and come all that way
with me,' I protested. 'It will do some other time.'

'Indeed, I must so,' she insisted. 'It's no distance at all,' and turning to her guests she blandly instructed them to carry on with their strupak while she 'sorted Miss Peckwitt'. 'I'll be back with you in a wee minute just,' she promised them.

'Aye, aye', her friends responded with equal blandness though they must have known that the 'wee minute just' would very likely be the best part of two hours.

I walked on, my eyes on the ground, mapping out my path to avoid the hazards of tussocks, boulders, rabbit-holes and boggy patches. A snipe rose suddenly from almost beneath my feet, startling me into a brief nerve-jangling sweatiness. I paused to take a breath and watch but the bird was out of sight before I could trace the erratic line of its flight. There came a trilling, bubbling sound as two cuckoos chased each other along a line of ancient fence posts that had at one time marked some now forgotten boundary. The cuckoos seemed in no way perturbed by my presence. Resuming my journey I began to work out times and reckoned that even if Willy had started to load immediately on his return it was going to be close to midnight before all my peats would be unloaded back at the cottage. It had been a long and tiring day but the prospect of a substantial part of my winter fuel being soon accessible within the walls of my croft spurred me on. I panted to myself the fragments of a Scottish dance tune and tried to walk in time to it. The breeze was cool now and had brought up goose-pimples on my scratched arms. The pads of my fingers felt hot and raw. Examining them I promised myself a lazy evening when I would contrive to spare enough water for bathing, shampooing and a manicure.

Looking up for a moment I espied Morag coming towards me. She was carrying two milk pails and she was carrying them as if they were both full.

'You've milked your cow!' I accused her.

We had all taken our milk pails with us so that we could go straight to the cows as soon as the peat loading was finished.

'Aye,' agreed Morag. 'An' yours too to save you goin' back for it.'

'But where's the lorry?' I demanded.

'Ach, he's away with it, mo ghaoil. Did he no tell you?'

'Away home?' I was aghast. 'But what about my peats? He was supposed to be coming back to load them.'

'He sent over a message sayin' he'd come back in a day or two for yours when the moors was a bitty drier,' Morag explained kindly. 'He said he'd never get near them now.'

'But he didn't send a message to me,' I retorted angrily.

'Ach, he was sayin' you looked so tired I daresay he hadn't the heart to tell you,' she said.

I had been tired but now I was cross in addition and this plod to the moors only to learn that I was not to get my peats loaded after all did nothing to lessen either my tiredness or my temper.

'He could have told me,' I said bitterly.

'But surely the man gave you a wee hint that he wasn't comin' back? Are you quite sure he said nothin' to you?'

I recollected my drive back with Willy. He had been intent on avoiding the worst of the boulders and potholes in the track and I had been glad of the respite from work so conversation had been monosyllabic until his attention had been caught by a couple of dinghies bobbing on the rippling water not far out from the shore.

'It looks as if the mackerel's in,' he had observed with sudden animation.

'Mm, I suppose so,' I was too tired to display more than a degree of interest.

'It looks as though they're after fillin' the boat,' said Willy enviously.

The Bruach crofters were fishermen as opposed to anglers. They liked to catch a lot of fish at one time—'to fill the boat' as they termed it and the conventional greeting to a man returning from an hour or two's fishing was 'An' is your fingers sore, then?', the implication being that he had caught so many fish the task of taking them off the hooks had made his fingers sore.

During the winter months the crofters were content enough with their salt herring though occasionally they admitted that their 'teeths' were 'waterin' for the taste of a fresh soo-yan'. In winter, however, fish were scarce in Bruach waters and even on the few calm days when no storms or aftermath of storms prevented the launching of the boats the men were loath to go to all the trouble of untying their dinghies; emptying them of the heavy stones which had ballasted them against the gales, and then dragging them down the rough shore when as like as not they would return after a couple of hours of chilly searching with no fish or perhaps with one or two very small ones to recompense them for their trouble; with the prospect of having to haul the dinghy above the highest high-tide line, replace the stones and re-tie the innumerable ropes that secured it. Thus it was that when spring brought the discernible presence of 'smollak' to be followed by 'soo-yan', 'lythe' and, later, shoals of mackerel, excitement rippled over the whole village. Boats were 'sorted'; zealously hoarded lumps of lead or rusty iron were ferreted out to be used as sinkers, and ancient fishing lines and corks were retrieved from the bilges.

As the lorry jolted homewards I had watched the two dinghies, trying to identify the shapes of the busy occupants and wondering if I should be lucky enough to find a fry of mackerel hanging on the doorhandle of my cottage next morning.

'Indeed, I could be doin' with a mackerel for my supper,' said Willy Ruag yearningly.

'You eat them, then?' I asked. An unquestioning submission to rubric made the majority of Bruachites averse to eating mackerel. They enjoyed catching it in quantity but mostly it was salted down for use as bait in lobster creels.

'Aye, so long as they're straight from the sea,' he replied.

'I'm hoping there'll be one for my breakfast tomorrow,' I said.

'For your breakfast?' His tone was scathing. 'Ach, what good will a mackerel be by breakfast time? You need to eat it within a couple of hours of it leavin' the sea, or it's no good at all.'

'If they're in by midnight it'll only be about eight hours to my breakfast time,' I pointed out.

'Ach, keep a mackerel more than four hours an' it's done for,' he retorted. I thought of town fish slabs where twelve- and twenty-four hour mackerel lay like stiff, faded replicas of the sinuous, irridescent fish we knew.

'Just imagine,' I said, and enthusiasm crept into my voice despite an immediate lack of appetite. 'A couple of fillets, dipped in oatmeal and salt and cooked through in the pan in their own oil.'

'They fairly makes my teeths water,' said Willy.

As I retraced our conversation enlightenment dawned and I knew that I should have accepted this last remark as Willy's oblique but courteous Highland way of telling me that he was going fishing and that I and my peats could wait until he was prepared to resume loading.

'That'll be my fine fellow now,' said Morag, drawing my attention to a third dinghy which was being rowed out from

the shore. The laggard afterglow of the sunset picked out a
fiery red head.

'Blast him!' I said.

Gaels invariably find a display of irritation amusing and
there was a glint in Morag's eyes as she said: 'Ach, I doubt
he'll give you a good fry of fish to make up for it.' I took my
full pail from her and realising that at least I did not have
to trek out to the moors again was full of gratitude.

The placatory string of fish was delivered to me next
morning via Erchy. Willy and his lorry did not appear in
the village again for some weeks. By then the Highland cattle,
many of which seemed to have something of the Spanish
bull in their make-up, had played toreadors with my peat
stacks, scattering the peats over the moor which, after the
rains of July, had resumed its normal sogginess. I rebuilt the
stacks and the cattle returned to the assault. Almost every
other day it rained. In desperation I rang up the coal
merchant and pleaded with him to send me a couple of tons
of coal.

Winter Fuel

THE first two weeks of June went by giving us fourteen days of uninterrupted sunshine. The skin of the moor tautened to a ringing hardness that resounded to the drumbeat of our footsteps. The stunted sedges were toasted brown and crisp so that they flaked beneath our feet as we trod. The April-burned heather was scratchy in its brittleness and all except the deepest bogs were at the stage of shedding a curling layer of peat. And still the sun shone. Young lambs bleated on the hills and wild-eyed calves, confined from birth to gloomy byres, were now coaxed out and tethered on the crofts where, for the first few days, they loudly protested their bewilderment at the new vista of space and light. Constantly on the verge of panic they cavorted within the restraining radius of the rope at any sudden movement such as the flight of a bird or the too close presence of a stalking cat. The hill ponies made for the higher ridges of the moor where, illogical as it may seem, greener and moister grazing could be found. There, as if striving consciously for effect, they strung themselves out in a graceful frieze against the skyline. Around the shore parties of eider ducks gossiped their exclamatory, inquisitive way; schools of porpoises tumbled about the glittering sea. Over it all the skylarks poured their jubilance, interspersed with the repetitive 'plunk' of diving gannets, the sound of which reached the shore exactly like the sound of heavy planks of wood being dropped one upon another.

On the crofts the oats were through, giving a silvery green bloom to the patches of harrowed earth. The earlier planted potatoes were already showing squat posies of green leaves and among them the crofters worked away with their hoes. The younger men took off their jackets and jerseys, for once unashamed to show their braces and striped union shirts. The more daring of them left open the two top buttons of their shirts revealing a 'V' of sun-scorched throat. Even the old folk—and by old I mean the septuagenarians onward —began to look thinner and younger as the sun flushed their wrinkles and encouraged them to discard a little of their winter padding. I myself, feeling relatively lissome for being dressed in thin garments that had lain so long at the bottom of a trunk that I had almost forgotten I possessed them, laboured to finish the outstanding work of my croft; clearing the debris of last year's stacks and gathering stray stones from among the grass so that they should not damage the scythe when the time for hay harvest came. Every night I contrasted the deepening tan on my hands and arms with the paler less exposed parts of my body. The mirror showed me streaks of bleached hair above a complexion which caused Morag to comment that I looked like a 'summer tinker'. Most comforting of all was the warm glow which had replaced the chill that had been biting deep between my shoulder blades all winter.

The time had come, Morag called to inform me, for us to think once again about transporting our peats home. 'Not that you have many,' she went on, although I thought I had cut an enormous quantity. 'You could maybe carry them home yourself.'

I had tried very determinedly one year to accustom myself to the incessant trudgings to and from the moors carrying home creelful after creelful of peats on my back, joining the procession of grandmothers and grandfathers and even young children who daily coped with their high-piled creels. Bent forward, with arms folded and the thick rope tight across their chests, they negotiated the stepping stones of the burn and called greetings and encouragement to me on rasping breaths. But my body rebelled against such exertion. My shoulders ached excruciatingly after every load and continued to ache for days afterwards. I unhesitatingly agreed to join once again in the hire of the lorry.

Morag left me to make the arrangements and soon returned to tell me that Willy Ruag would be coming the very next morning 'if the Lord spares him' to transport our peats.

In view of my experience the previous year it was agreed
that mine should be the first to be loaded.

'Let's hope the weather holds,' I said without a trace of
pessimism. The sky was still blue and cloudless except for
tiny pennants of white that hardly changed their shape however long one looked. The hills were tranquil under a peach
bloom of haze.

'Ach, they're after sayin' there's no sign of a break in it
yet a whiley,' Morag confirmed. 'An' you know yon beasts
we call 'Reudan' an' that you say is 'woodlice'?'

I nodded.

'Well, the children's shakin' them in their hands every
mornin' an' they're not rollin' themselves up like they do
when it's goin' to rain.'

This particular method of weather prediction made me
shudder. Morag saw my grimace.

'They're as good at tellin' the weather as them meteoritists
anyway,' she said defensively.

Next day I was waiting at the gate of the croft when the
lorry halted outside and with a loud honking which was
patently unnecessary summoned me to join the bevy of loaders
who were already ensconced in the back. All the women
carried a milk pail and doubtless theirs, like mine, contained
a 'piece' for their lunch. The track was dry, the moor was
dry and the lorry romped alongside the peat stacks. Immediately we began loading. There was no breeze today to
avert the vicious attacks of the clegs and they banqueted on
any exposed flesh. Everyone wore gumboots. Everyone that
is except myself, for I, hating the idea of heavy boots on
such a warm day, was wearing sandals on my bare feet.
There is no part of the human body that is distasteful to a
cleg and it was lucky that I had tied the ankles of my slacks
with string. As it was they assaulted me through the holes

of my sandals and probed deep into my unprotected arms and neck. The Bruachites seemed to have become immune to the attacks of these creatures but I was tortured by them; forced to frequent exclamation and slapping them into bloody patches on my skin.

'What's the matter with Miss Peckwitt?' someone asked.

'Ach, the beasts is at her,' explained Erchy, who was one of the loaders.

Perhaps I should explain that in Bruach the term 'beast' embraced the whole of the insect and most of the animal world. 'A beast is at her' could mean that the victim was being gored by a bull or merely suffering the discomfort of a few midge bites. Only the difference in tone betrayed the degree of calamity.

When all my own peats were loaded and home it was the turn for Morag's stacks to be attended to but first she insisted on a strupak. Already she had lit a fire of heather and peat in a hollow left by an ancient hag and soon the kettle was boiling. She threw a couple of handfuls of tea into it and Erchy drew a few squirts of milk from the most acquiescent cow in reach. We sat on the warm turf and ate our 'pieces'.

'My, but it's too hot to eat,' said Erchy, sipping a steaming mug of tea. The taut burned skin of his face shone with sweat.

'My but it's hot, hot, hot,' moaned Nelly Elly, holding her damp blouse away from under her arms.

I lay on my tummy listening to the competitive exuberance of the larks; to the rarer notes of the tiring cuckoo; to the elusive raspings of a corncrake.

'The trouble with this sort of weather is that nobody can think of any other tropical conversation than that it's too hot,' complained Morag. 'Is there not somethin' else that is worth talkin' about?'.

Erchy made some inarticulate comment and stretched himself flat on his back.

'Now if we was wearin' trousers like Erchy an' Miss Peckwitt we could lie down too,' said Nelly Elly with a provocative glance at old Sarah. Sarah was a vintage spinster, very missionary conscious and unique in that she was reputedly a virgin.

'Here, here,' Sarah reproached her and giving a coy giggle she tucked her long skirts primly over her ankles. 'Don't be after sayin' things like that.'

'Those trousers Miss Peckwitt is wearin' is very good to her,' Morag hastened to defend me, though privately she disapproved of women in slacks.

'I'd be afraid of bein' killed in them,' said Sarah. She blushed, obviously finding the conversation immodest.

I laughed. 'Why should you be killed just because you're wearing slacks?'

'No, not like that,' Sarah hastened to explain. 'But what I mean is, if I was to die suddenly an' me wearin' trousers how would I face the Lord an' Him not knowin' whether I was a girl or a boy?'

Erchy sat up. 'Well, I can tell you, you're not either,' he told her scornfully. 'An' as near eighty as you are He's not likely to care anyway.'

'Me, near eighty?' Sarah's indignant tone quelled the shocked reproaches that Nelly Elly and Morag had begun to utter. 'I'm nowhere near eighty I'll have you know, my fine fellow,' she told him.

'You must be,' retorted Erchy, winking at us.

'Indeed I am not,' reiterated Sarah. 'I am no more than seventy-eight.'

No-one laughed. There was not even a smile. Morag said, 'Aye well, work doesn't get done by itself.' We stood up, caressing tired backs, and started to dismantle the next stack.

'How noisy it is today,' I observed as the sound of the lorry spread itself over the normally silent moors. 'What with the larks singing and our chattering and the lorry roaring away it's not a bit like the lonely quiet place it usually is.'

'Indeed an' I'm glad of that,' said Nelly Elly. 'I hate it just when the cattle go so far away that there isn't a body or a house in sight when I go to do the milking.' Nelly Elly rose earlier than the rest of us and had usually returned from the morning milking before there was more than a wisp of smoke to be discerned in the village. As a consequence it was always Nelly Elly who had the lonely task of locating the cattle which, during the night, might have roamed miles away from their evening grazing. The more slothful milkers had only to enquire of her in which direction they should go to seek their cattle.

'Miss Peckwitt loves to be on the moors by herself,' Morag asserted playfully. 'Is that not true?' she asked me.

I smiled confirmation. My wanders on the Bruach moors provided me with hours of pleasure both by day and in the evening when with the lamp drawn close to my books on birds and plants I could try to identify what I had seen and collected.

'Indeed you shouldn't do too much of that,' cautioned Erchy. 'These moors would send a body mad if you took too much to do with them on your own. Especially when the mist comes down. Even the birds goes crazy when it's misty,' he added.

I grinned unconcernedly. Being caught out on the moors in a sudden mist was not particularly pleasant but it had once given me an unforgettable experience. I had been crouched under Bonny milking her when the mist had swirled

in with dramatic suddenness. As I had been stripping the
last teatful into the pail I had looked up and there directly
above me hovered a bemused kestrel so close that I could
look through the exquisite tracery of its spread wings. Its
stillness and silence were uncanny and for a moment I
thought that I was its prey. Then Bonny gave an impatient
jerk of her head and the kestrel flew into the mist, leaving
me with the memory of what I felt was likely to be an
unrepeated experience.

My indifference to Erchy's warnings spurred him on to
more cautionary tales.

'There's old Donald Bhan, now. He spends too much time
by himself whether it's on the moors or at home, an' he was
actin' awful queer when I saw him at his stacks the other day.'

We all looked at Erchy expectantly.

'He didn't see me comin' so I hid behind a stack an'
watched him. He had his peat iron an' his spade an' a fork
an' a stripper all stuck into the ground in front of him, an'
there he was like a sergeant major shoutin' orders at them.
"Attention!" he barks. "Eyes right! Shoulder rifles!" It's as
true as I'm here, he was drillin' them as though he had an
army in front of him. I let him do it for a while an' then I
went close up behind him an' shouted "HALT!" in my
loudest voice. My God! but he got a shock, I can tell you.
His mouth dropped open so wide I thought his teeth would
be fallin' into the bog.'

We all laughed, though Morag, seeming to be a little
embarrassed on Donald's behalf, ended her laughter with
murmured sympathy.

'Maybe we'd all have time to play at the peats if we had
a cart,' I pointed out.

'How would that help him?' demanded Erchy, looking
puzzled.

'Well, having a cart means he can get his peats home in his own time. He doesn't have to carry them himself or wait for a lorry like the rest of us.'

'I'm not gettin' your meanin',' said Erchy, still puzzled.

'His peats—in his cart. He has a cart, hasn't he?' I repeated testily.

'He has two or three but I don't see how they'd help him get home his peats,' said Erchy.

'Miss Peckwitt's meanin' to say a carrrt,' interpreted Morag.

Erchy's face cleared. 'Ach, is that it? I thought she was goin' mad herself talkin' about a cat helpin' him to get home the peats. Honest, you English folk do speak a funny language sometimes.'

The lorry returned for its next load and brought Katy who had decided to join us in the hire so as to have her own peats taken home. Katy was Bruach's newest bride, having married Fergus only two years previously. Wherever she went she still had to endure bawdy innuendoes about her married state.

'Ach, but I'm often wishin' I'd married myself,' old Sarah confided to me during one lull in our work and when no-one else was in earshot.

'Do you, Sarah?' I asked with some surprise. She had always seemed to me to be a very contented and self-sufficient old lady. Certainly I had never dreamed that she might have been pining for a husband.

'Oh, aye,' she admitted with a little shamefaced sigh. 'Many's the time, even now, I would jump at the offer of a man if I got it.'

'You seem to have manag⸱ ⸱ very well without one,' I comforted her.

'Oh, yes indeed. It's not for livin' with I'd be wantin' him but it's for when I go places an' I'm all by myself.' She sighed again and resumed with touching pathos. 'It's then I get the feelin' that I'd like a man of my own beside me, just to take the bare look off me.'

The loading progressed with continued chaff and merriment until about nine o'clock when the driver remembered he had a date. He rushed off, promising to return the following morning to resume work—'if the Lord spares me,' he threw as a parting shot at Morag.

We pulled moss and with it wiped our peat-dusty hands and faces. We gathered up some of the small broken pieces of peat that were too crumbly to stack and yet were precious for lighting a fire and filled the sack each one of us had brought with us, tied them with rope and slung them over our shoulders. Loaded with full pails and sacks we converged again into an attenuated line and plodded home at a companionably slow pace, each of us evincing a degree of tiredness that varied inversely with age. Old Sarah blithely talked of making a dumpling when she got home and a dumpling takes three to four hours for the boiling.

The heat of the day was over but the sun-baked rocks on either side of the track gave out patches of their stored warmth. The burn rippled with a childish trill in contrast with its full-throated winter roar; the water of the bay was purple-shadowed, patched with all the colours of a bunch of delphiniums. Overhead a tern flew, an eel hanging from its beak being plainly discernible.

'See that now,' said Erchy. 'It's away to its nest. I've seen it near every night around this time an' it's never without an eel in its beak.' I leaned against a rock, resting my load as I watched the bird disappear over the ridge of the moor. It was the third evening in succession I myself had seen it flying thus.

'Indeed an' I'll be glad to see my own nest tonight,' said Morag.

'Me too,' agreed Katy fervently. 'The sooner I get to my bed the better I'll be pleased.'

'Ach, you an' Fergy can never wait to get to bed,' Erchy taunted her amid a burst of anticipatory laughter. Katy's glowing face glowed even deeper.

Old Sarah was suddenly serious. 'Aye, but it's sad I am to see there's no sign of a bairn with you yet,' she observed regretfully, her eyes assessing Katy's slim body.

Katy's face assumed an enigmatic smile. She stared up at the navy-blue cloud that was waiting to engulf the sunset.

'But never mind,' continued Sarah reassuringly. 'I've no doubt when the Lord sees fit for you to have a bairn then the Lord will put a bairn in your belly, I doubt.'

Erchy stopped in his tracks and thinking he had noticed something unusual we too stopped. 'Well,' he said, shaking his head in a puzzled way, 'that's the first time I ever heard Fergus referred to as the "Lord".'

He glanced briefly at the range of expressions on our faces, then doubtless anxious to escape the reproof that threatened he turned his back on us and went quickly ahead.

'Oidhche mhath!' he called over his shoulder in a tight voice.

'Oidhche mhath!' we returned uncertainly.

Venison Supper

Down on the shore the men were working on their boats. Some tended small fires of driftwood over which cans of tar were being heated; others wielded saws and adzes, chisels and hammers. They greeted me abstractedly, only briefly interrupting their boat talk with its references to tumble-home and garboard strakes; to stern tubes and fairleads; to

stems and aprons—enchanting names which at one time had
been completely unintelligible to me but which now I could
precisely identify. I paused beside Erchy's dinghy and
watched him slathering melted tar into seams and cracks
which showed through the thick, blistered coating that had
been built up over the years.

'More tar!' I commented with a grimace. If Erchy took
me out in his dinghy I was expected to help haul it up and
down the beach and tar makes a boat exceedingly heavy.

'Aye.'

'Is it necessary to do the boat every year?' I pursued.

'Aye,' he said again. 'Two weeks of June sun does more
harm to a boat than two years in and out of the water.' He
rammed the black sticky brush into the gap between two
boards. 'See that now?' he asked. 'That's just the last few
days that's opened that up. If I was to put her into the sea
without tarring her the water would pour in, just.'

My experience of Erchy's dinghy had taught me that
despite the tar the sea usually did pour into her. I was used
to spending a lot of my time bailing.

'I hear Hamish was after tryin' to sell you his new boat
that he bought last year,' he said, straightening up and
wiping the sleeve of his pullover across his fiery cheeks.

'Was he?' I exclaimed. 'When?'

'Aye, so he was sayin'.' Erchy was positive. 'The other
night, just. He came to see you specially.'

I have never ceased to be astonished by the wiliness of the
Bruachites. In my innocence I had been under the impression
that Hamish had called to ask if I could sell him a hive of
bees. I said as much to Erchy.

'What would Hamish be wantin' with a hive of bees?'
His tone was derisive. 'You should have known better.'

'Well, that's all he talked about,' I returned limply.

'Ach, he'd make damty sure before ever he mentioned it
that you couldn't sell him a hive of bees.' He reflected a
moment. 'Are you sure he made no mention of his boat at all?'

'Not until he was leaving. Then he just said something
about my needing a nice lightweight boat so that I could go
fishing whenever I felt like it.'

'An' did you agree with him?'

'Yes.'

'Well, then, I doubt he thinks he's made a bargain with
you.' Erchy slapped on more tar.

'I certainly didn't say anything about buying his boat,' I
said anxiously. 'I can't possibly afford it yet.'

Erchy carefully placed the can of tar on the fire. 'An'
supposin' you could afford a boat yon's no good to you. Not
if you've any sense,' he confided. I waited for enlightenment.
'He got that boat at the beginnin' of last year an' then he
went away to a job an' he just left her there on the beach
without nothin' so much as done to her at all.' There was
strong disapproval in his voice and expression. 'This year
when he tried to put her in the sea she was just like a colander.
The only reason he thinks it right to try an' sell her to you is
because he knows you can swim.'

'Well, thanks for telling me,' I said, realising that the
decision to warn me and thus betray his friend must for him
have been a much considered one. 'I'll remember to be
careful what I say next time he comes to try to buy a hive
of bees.'

'You'll no say I told you.' It was a statement, not a
question, and he needed no reply. He dipped the brush into
the can and then held it poised so that a line of black
scribbled itself over the stones. 'I don't see him ever sellin'
the boat hereabouts,' he said. 'The only way he's likely to
get rid of her is by puttin' her in the papers.'

The sea was calm; the tide was well out and I picked my
way down to the shore and waded into the shallow water,
intent on collecting carragheen moss to dry in preparation
for making jellies and puddings. The moss grew on craggy
sea-washed boulders which were exposed only at low tides
and the more inaccessible the boulder the more nutritious
the moss was considered to be. It was a congenial task for a
perfect day. The sea washed languidly around my gumbooted
feet; the smell of the barnacle-stippled tangle was fresh and
strong. Convinced that I could feel the beneficial effect of
every lungful I practised taking long deep breaths while I
wrenched handfuls of moss from the abrasive rocks. When
my bag was full I bent to dip my bleeding knuckles in the
sea. The water was crystal clear and I could see the long
thick stems of sea-wrack genuflecting with the lazy surge of
the tide. Deeper down grew the secret jungle of other weeds
in which no doubt all specimens of sea life awaited their prey.
There would be lobsters, I knew, and crabs and perhaps a
conger eel threading its sinuous way. I recalled the piece of
chart from an echo-sounder which Angus, the fisherman, had
once brought me and which stayed pinned to my kitchen
wall for many weeks. The tints of the chart varied according
to the atmosphere from a dark sepia to a paleness that
left the outlines scarcely distinguishable, but on its sepia days
it revealed the, to me unsuspected, peaks and valleys that
make up the sea bed. It had never struck me until then that
the sea conceals a land as rugged as the land we see. Angus
had pointed out small smudges of sepia and interpreted them
as shoals of fish. One shape of smudge showed the herring
they were seeking; another showed a shoal of mackerel which
was of little commercial value; yet another he distinguished
as being 'horse mackerel'—a fish they cursed not just because
of its unsaleability but because its sharp fins made it difficult

to shake out of the net. Eventually the piece of chart had
faded permanently but while it was there it had proved as
much a source of interest to my town friends as if it had been
an expensively acquired painting.

I looked up as I heard a faint quacking and saw a proud
shelduck appear leading her newly hatched family on an
exploratory tour among the rocks. The drake followed and
was the first to discern my presence. With husky warnings he
ushered his mate and brood away. A little farther out a great
northern diver rested on the water, seemingly motionless
except when it lifted its beak to utter its strange wild cry.
Each spring the solitary bird, known locally as 'the Widow',
came to the bay to wait expectantly for the mate which
Tearlaich had shot three years previously. Each year it
lingered long after the experts claimed it should have left
our shores. Even as I watched she lifted her beak and the
haunting despair of her cry was strangely affecting. The
Bruachites were touched by the constancy of the bird and
Tearlaich had to endure acrid references to his cruelty.

'It was good eatin',' he defended himself. 'An' it's daft to
feel like that when a bird's good for the pot.'

'There's folks that say it's ill luck to kill them,' they
warned him.

'Ach, that's nonsense.' Tearlaich tried to make his voice
sound indifferent but despite the remaining bird offering
itself as a perfect target he never made any attempt to shoot
it. If he was working near the shore and the diver's
sudden cry startled him he would jump and mutter male-
diction.

Though there was no perceptible rise in the line of water
around the rocks I knew the tide had turned. Living and
working in close proximity to the sea one acquires an aware-
ness of such things, so that a change of tide is more of a

sensation than a observation. I sensed that there was a sort
of brio, a small stirring of excitement in the water; that the
slight breeze blew fractionally cooler on my skin. There
was a new alertness in the attitudes of the sea birds which
hitherto had been basking and preening themselves on the
guano-spattered rocks; the excitement communicated itself
to the life in the shallow pools far above the tide; tiny crabs
heaved themselves out from the shell debris while sea
anemones, which contracted looked like red sweets that had
been sucked and spat out, now blossomed into rosettes of
tentacles in expectation of their prey.

Slowly I made my way up the shore. The warm rocks were
speckled with winkles whose shells had bleached grey in the
sun. I flicked off several, sending them to join their inky
black kindred in the pools. I picked up a few stems of the
seaweed which the Bruachites referred to as 'staff' and examined them. At the right stage of ripeness the weed was
supposed to be very refreshing and Bruach children liked to
munch a piece of 'staff' as town children liked to munch a
bar of nougat. But first it must be washed ashore. After a
summer storm the children would search along the line of
sea-wrack looking for a stem which had embedded in its pith
a particular kind of sea snail. Like the farmer who main-
tains that the best cheese in his dairy is invariably the one
the mouse will choose, so the children claimed that the
sweetest stems of 'staff' were the ones the snails liked to feast
on. The stems I picked up were dry and untempting and I
threw them down again.

The men were still working at their boats but with less
dedication now. Erchy was wiping his tarry hands on a
bundle of wet seaweed. He acknowledged me with a nod.

'A lovely evening for a sail,' I observed in passing.

'Aye, well, if that's what you've a mind for you'd get with

Hector. He's to take that lady tourist for a run to Rhuna as
soon as the tide's up far enough.'

I shook my head, having no mind to go. Rhuna was some
miles away and having met the tourist in question I knew her
to be irrepressibly garrulous. It is not only to the watcher on
the shore that a small boat appears to diminish in size as it
moves out to sea: the occupants are also aware that its
confinity increases in proportion to the distance from the
land and that any incompatibility among them will increase
correspondingly. I did not seek an invitation from Hector
but instead continued my scramble along the shore in
search of whatever treasure I should be lucky enough to
find.

The island beaches were a repository for every kind of
flotsam and jetsam and there were few crofters who did not
make a point of roaming the shores several times a week
retrieving wood or other objects, some of whose legitimate
use they were completely ignorant but which were salvaged
because they might be of some conceivable use in the future.
Every croft had its hoard and even if an object was not
considered worth carrying home it was at least dragged up
above high tide in case it should be needed at some time.
And how often it was needed! Apart from firewood we found
iron bolts and shackles and chains; hinges and odd pieces of
metal which even if you had had access to a store you would
have found it impossible to buy. We found drums of kapok
with which we stuffed cushions and quilts; brushes and
brooms; lengths of rope; tins of grease and drums of
petroleum jelly. There were pieces of cork of every size and
shape; oars and boathooks; enormous hatch-covers and pit-
props for building; crates and boxes of every description. We
found coir fenders which, if one could resist the importun-
ings of the boat owners, made excellent pouffes, and the

children had firework celebrations whenever bundles of cordite and smoke floats were washed ashore.

I gathered a good bundle of wood, roped it on my back and was about to make for home when I saw an interesting looking object a little further along the shore. Going to investigate I found it to be the washed-up carcase of a young stag. There was no visible sign of injury and I stood pondering how it had got into the sea in the first place. I heard a shout behind me. Yawn came hurrying up. He turned the beast over with his foot and we saw then the great sea-washed gash in its throat.

'My, my, but that's a fine beast you have there.' His tone sounded congratulatory. 'A fine beast indeed,' he repeated, 'an' not more than a few hours in the water at that.'

'How would it have got there?' I asked him.

'Ach, fightin', I'm thinkin'.' He nodded in the direction of the largest of the outlying islands. 'There's that many of them over there an' they get to fightin'.' He butted his head towards me in imitation of an angry stag. 'This one must have got the worst of it an' gone away back till it was over the cliff an' into the sea,' he explained. He bent down, examining the carcase more closely and then he looked up at me.

'You'll not get it home like this,' he said. 'I'd best skin it for you.' I murmured a doubtful 'Yes, please,' and let myself think of the uses of deer skin. He whipped out his knife and made a long slit in the belly. I turned away seaward as his hands plunged inside and detached the guts. There was a splash as the guts landed in the sea in front of me and I recoiled again.

'A fine beast,' Yawn mumbled again. I watched his deft handling of the knife as it slid under the skin. When he had finished he threw the skin towards me. 'Just you wash that in

the sea an' then you can dry it afterwards.' I did as I was
told and when I turned from my task I saw that the head of
the beast was off and he was already beginning to joint it.

'You'll not be needin' the butcher for a week or two at
this rate,' he complimented me.

I felt my mouth drop open.

'But Yawn,' I protested. 'It's not fit for eating, is it?'

'Not for a day or two,' he replied equably. 'You'll need
to hang it for a wee whiley an' then it will be ready.' He
glanced up, saw my expression and misinterpreting it
hastened to add: 'I'm tellin' you, its a young beast so it'll
not need much hanging. You could cook it maybe the day
after tomorrow.'

'But surely washed up venison isn't fit for people to eat?'
I argued weakly.

Yawn was an impatient man and his tongue could be
scathing on occasion. 'Not fit to eat?' In his horror he
dropped his knife and the sound of it clattering over the
stones was like a derisive echo. 'Of course it's fit to eat,
woman!' he bawled at me.

I felt I had to persist. 'But we don't know how long it's
been dead.' My voice was almost a wail.

Yawn retrieved his knife and gave me a look of complete
disdain. 'I tell you it's not more than a few hours has it been
in the sea an' do you not know, woman, that sea water is
salt water an' that salt water makes the best pickle?'

His contention sounded reasonable enough and I felt my
doubts receding a little.

'Won't you have some for yourself?' I suggested subtly.

'That's very good of you, Miss Peckwitt. Indeed I would
be very glad to have some. I'm very fond of a wee bitty
venison.'

His acceptance made me feel much better. 'Take as much as you like,' I told him graciously.

He stowed the joints in his own sack, roped it on his back and said he would carry it home for me. I rolled up the dripping skin and carried it myself.

At my cottage he dropped the sack and asked me where I wanted him to put the meat.

'I'll just take one haunch,' I said. 'You have the rest.'

His delight was obvious. 'Are you sure that's goin' to be enough for you?' he demanded.

I was quite sure.

He extracted a haunch and hung it for me in the outside cupboard. 'You'll enjoy that in a day or so,' he assured me as he left.

For two days the haunch hung there and whenever I opened the cupboard I eyed it dubiously wondering if I should ever pluck up courage to cook it.

On the third day I made an excuse to visit Yawn's house where his sister Sarah greeted me.

'My, my, but that's a grand lot of venison you gave my brother the other day just. We had it with our potatoes an' it was good. We fairly enjoyed it.'

'It was all right, was it?'

'Indeed I've never tasted better,' she enthused and looked at me for confirmation. 'Did you not have any yourself yet?'

I admitted I hadn't cooked my haunch yet but seeing her so hale and hearty I resolved that I would cook it for supper the very next evening when I was expecting Mary, my friend from England, to arrive. I told myself that the venison would probably be as wholesome as any meat I might be able to buy from the unsavoury little butcher's van which might or might not turn up next morning. I recollected the last purchase I had made from the gore-splashed van. The

customer before me had been buying mince and when the
butcher had come to serve me he had been unable to find
the cloth for wiping down his cutting board. He had looked
in the van and then on the road thinking he had dropped it.
We had both noticed a sheepdog pulling at a grey-looking
something a little distance away. With an oath the butcher
had rushed at the dog, wrested the cloth from it and then
had returned to wipe down the board with the cloth. So
inured had I become to this sort of thing I did not even
murmur a complaint.

The following afternoon I took down the haunch and
wrapped it in a pastry case, as advised by Mrs. Beeton. I put
it into the oven to cook slowly for several hours. By the time
Mary arrived the whole house was full of a tempting aroma.

'My Golly! That smells good!' was Mary's first remark.
And a little while later it was: 'Becky, how long is supper
going to be?'

Debating whether or not to tell her anything of its history I
lifted the haunch from the oven and broke off the crust. The
meat tin was half full of rich brown gravy. I placed the
haunch on a willow-patterned dish and carried it to the
table. Beside it I placed a tin of corned beef. Mary, who by
this time was sniffing ecstatically, looked up enquiringly. I
ignored her and took up the carving knife. It slid through
the flesh as effortlessly as if it had been the breast of a young
chicken. Mary held out her plate. I took a deep breath.

'I think I ought to tell you . . .' I began. Mary listened and
drew back her plate. 'Yawn and Sarah have eaten it,' I
ended. 'And they're all right.' She still held on to her plate.

'Aren't you even going to taste it?' I asked anxiously.

'Not until you've tasted it first,' she said.

I picked up a slice in my fingers and nibbled it. I pushed
the rest of the slice into my mouth and licked my fingers

before forking several more slices on to my own plate. Mary took a small piece and ate it.

'It's delicious!' she said incredulously and proffered her plate again. Across the table we grinned at each other and took up our knives and forks. I had a sudden thought and put mine down again.

'Just a minute, Mary,' I said. 'Don't you think this is one occasion when we can't neglect to say grace?'

We bowed our heads.

Romance

WE were gathered in the schoolhouse for a meeting with the landlord and a representative of the Department of Agriculture who wished to sound village opinion with regard to a proposal for realigning croft boundaries. The scheme purported to be for the benefit of the village but the crofters, always suspicious of anything new, were intent on vetoing any change. They did not see how realignment could take place without robbing one man to give to another. Someone was bound to lose, they asserted, and as every man present was determined it should not be himself there seemed little point in having a meeting at all. Nevertheless the crofters attended as they attended every meeting ever held in the village. It 'made a change', they said, and though outwardly they were prepared to treat a subject seriously one sensed the latent hope that some amusing argument or comic situation might develop during the discussion. They in fact regarded a 'meeting' as just a different kind of ceilidh with the presence of strangers making it necessary to restrain the impulse to comment or deride.

Tonight the presence of the landlord ensured that there would be little if any argument for though the Bruachites were fortunate in having a relatively tolerant and indulgent landlord there still lingered in their minds the vestiges of a feudal system where the goodwill of the landlord was necessary for survival. There was for instance either a law or a tradition that every male in the village should be given so many paid days' work on the estate every year and though times had changed and the crofters were prosperous enough not to need such benevolence they would have resented any suggestion that the practice be discontinued. The absence of an offer from the landlord of such work would be regarded as evidence that they were out of favour and this they were anxious to avoid.

So everyone listened to the speech of the Department representative in courteous silence. Everyone that is except Torquil who though he was a 'wee bit simple' was the possessor of a loud clear voice. It was these two attributes that made him the ideal choice for a heckler and having been well coached beforehand he now jumped up at regular intervals to bawl loudly 'We want our rights!'. The speaker bore with the constant interruptions good humouredly for a time but at last becoming exasperated he turned on Torquil. 'Very well, you insist you want your rights,' he taxed him. 'Tell me, what are your rights?'

Torquil's face went completely blank. 'I'm damned if I know,' he replied and sat down.

Soon afterwards the landlord, who must have known the futility of trying to make changes, brought the meeting to a close. His car whisked away the dispirited speaker before the audience had finally emerged from the schoolhouse.

'Oh, my, but it's a grand evenin',' said Anna Vic, looking out to sea.

It was indeed a grand evening. An evening that had followed a day that had been warm and sunny as a day of midsummer. The sea was lazy and patched at intervals with dimpled water that betrayed the presence of shoals of 'sooyan'. Every few minutes we would see the dimples break into silver and would hear the lisp of water as the shoal leaped to evade the pursuit of predatory lythe. A mile or so out from the shore a rabble of gulls hovered restlessly above the sea, their bickering, protesting cries sounding thin as they reached us on the slight, sea-cooled breeze. Swinging lazily out at her mooring lay Hector's motor boat, newly painted and refurbished in readiness for the tourists who as yet were arriving only sporadically.

'Seein' we're dressed,' said Erchy (which meant that some of us were wearing shoes instead of gumboots) 'what about a cruise?'

'Why not?' agreed Hector. There was an immediate move to launch the dinghy.

'I'll need to tell Katy,' someone said.

'I'll need to see to the hens.'

There were so many people to be told and invited to come along; so many chores which needed to be done, that we arranged to meet at the shore in an hour's time. Knowing I could safely stretch the hour another ten minutes I did so but when I arrived at the shore only Hector and Erchy and Janet were there, sitting on the gunwale of the dinghy awaiting passengers.

'May as well put you two out,' said Hector and rowed us to the motor boat. We climbed aboard but Janet, whose eyes had at once begun to scan the land, suddenly seemed anxious.

'Is that no my cow there, Erchy?' she asked, pointing to an animal that was grazing perilously near to the steep cliff edge.

'Aye, so it is,' Erchy confirmed.

'Then I must get to her an' drive her away.' Janet started to climb back into the dinghy. 'Isn't that the place her own mother fell over only last spring?'

'It must be in the beast's nature,' said Hector.

'Nature or no, I'll need to get her away from that cliff,' insisted Janet. The two men rowed her ashore and I was left alone on the boat. I sat in the stern, listening to the music of the sea as it caressed the boat; peering down into the clear green-grey shoaly depths. I thought of ninety year old Donald, a pious and forthright man who would rather have cut off his right hand than tell a lie, yet who insisted that once in his youth he had seen a merman in these waters. Anyone but the virtuous Donald would have described it as being a mermaid but Donald, who would never have permitted himself to look upon a naked female form—even if it was only the top half—insisted that despite its breasts the creature was male. He had been about eighteen at the time, he used to say, and had been fishing lobster creels just around

the point when the merman had risen from the water about
fifty yards away from the boat. It had just stayed there,
watching him and Donald had stared transfixed until the
creature had seemed to stretch out an arm as if beckoning
him. Then Donald had taken fright. He let go of the creel and
grasping the oars started to row as fast as he could for home,
praying for guidance as he did so. Even I believed Donald's
story, having read that there were reports of dugongs being
sighted in the past in the area.

Once again the dinghy came alongside. This time it was
full of people, a laughing happy crowd intent on enjoying
the evening. The dinghy returned for another load. There
was no limit to the number of passengers on an evening
cruise. The law was interpreted as limiting the number of
fare-paying passengers and as this was a free cruise for
friends only the limit was reached when the boatman considered the amount of freeboard to be over the danger limit.
Sometimes it could be a matter of inches.

Perhaps it is because the Hebrideans live so close to the
sea that they are, or appear to be, indifferent to its hazards.
A boatman may have some misgivings as to the capacity of
his boat but passengers seldom have any. As an instance I
recall a time when I was about to travel on the official ferry
to the island one wild and stormy day. When the boatmen
had come to untie the ropes that held her they saw that the
number of passengers greatly exceeded the number permitted
or considered safe. They had refused to sail until some disembarked. No one had made any move. The boatmen were
adamant. The last twenty people aboard must get off and
wait for another ferry, they said. Still no-one moved.

'I'm no takin' this boat to sea loaded like this,' one had
insisted. 'She's no safe. You can see for yourselves how
little free board there is. She'll never make the other side.'

An old man had objected. 'We're on board now,' he said stubbornly. 'How can you force us to get off?'

'I'm sayin' she's overloaded an' dangerous,' reiterated the boatman. 'An' some of you will need to get ashore.'

'There's none of us gettin' ashore,' the old man had told him. 'An' what's more, with the tide goin' out like it is you'll need to sail from here or you'll have her bangin' her bottom out.'

The boatman looked harassed. There was no disputing the truth of the statement and he looked as if he might soon yield to persuasion. Grudgingly he begun to untie the rope from the bollard.

In a mounting panic I had pushed my way forward. If the boatman considered it unsafe I was not disposed to argue. 'I'm getting off,' I said, but as I was about to jump ashore the old man restrained me with a hand on my arm. 'Don't give in to him, madam,' he instructed. 'You have every right to be here. You were one of the first ones aboard.'

'I don't want to be one of the first ones to drown, though,' I retorted. 'I'm waiting for the next boat.'

The old man had seemed very disappointed by what he no doubt considered to be my treachery and only two other passengers—both of them tourists—followed my example. The boat had sailed, overcrowded as she was, and reached the other side safely. I imagined the triumph of the old man.

The last dinghy load came out. In addition to Morag and Anna Vic and Niall it contained three American girls who had arrived in the village only that evening. Already Hector had appropriated the attention of one of them, a pretty blonde.

'Here, look after that for a minute,' Niall said, taking off his wooden leg and throwing it to me. With only one good leg Niall was as agile on land or sea as any man with two. He always referred to his wooden leg as his 'spare leg'.

'Okay, start her up,' he instructed Hector and went forward to cast off the mooring. Niall though owning a croft in Bruach spent little of his time in the village, being mostly away on a variety of jobs. When he was at home he seemed to consider that the whole village was in need of his care and attention.

There was rarely any preconceived plan or intended destination for these impromptu evening cruises. The passengers were content to sing and chatter while allowing the helmsman to steer in any direction he fancied. Mostly we just wandered about the sea, perhaps towards caves or a cove that looked interesting. Occasionally we landed to explore some spot that was relatively inaccessible by land or perhaps finding ourselves near a harbour of one of the islands we would go ashore and descend on a household— always there was a claim to kinship—where we would enjoy a ceilidh. It was no hardship for a household to have a party of say twenty to thirty people arriving around midnight without warning. Rather it was the reverse. In the lonely places of the Hebrides a hostess regards it as an honour for her home to be chosen by visitors and it is she on parting who thanks the guests for partaking of her hospitality. The moment the presence of a boatload of people was discerned near the harbour the kettle would go on the fire, a batch of girdle scones prepared and hopefully a male member of the house would make quickly for the shore to claim the privilege of offering entertainment.

Tonight, Niall took over the helm Hector being too busy with his blonde to have time for attending to his boat. It soon became plain that Niall was taking us towards a small isolated bay where a tumbling burn edged with a white frill the skirts of a range of black craggy hills, dividing them from a tiny acreage of flat land and an opposing range of equally gaunt hills. A bothy built to house the river watchers stood near the river bank, its negligible chimney busy with smoke.

There was no landing place so Erchy blew expertly into a cow's horn to summon the launching of a dinghy to take us ashore. He blew several times before there was a sign of life. Then an old man appeared, waved exaggeratedly with both hands high above his head and came hurrying down to where the dinghy lay. He dragged it down to the water.

'That's watchers for you,' Johnny pointed out sarcastically. 'They're supposed to be keepin' an eye open for poachers an' here's us could have netted the lot in the time it's taken for him to see we're here.'

Hector lifted his head from the blonde's shoulder. 'I don't know why we didn't,' he said ruefully. 'Tsere's a net ready under tse floorboards.

'Whist!' Erchy cautioned him as the dinghy drew close. 'Padruig will hear you.'

Niall manoeuvred the boat as close inshore as the tide would permit to save lengthy ferrying and when all but he and Erchy and Hector were ashore it was suggested that we should go up to the house while they moored the boat at a safer distance from the shore. Erchy took over the dinghy while Padruig led us towards the bothy.

There was no doubting our welcome and we crowded into the cell-like bothy, with its bare wood walls and uncovered cement floor. Except for a rough plank bed beside the fire the only furniture was a table and three chairs all obviously contrived from driftwood. Along one wall of the room was a line of nearly full sacks containing oatmeal, flour, sugar and potatoes. On a low shelf stood several rusty biscuit tins, doubtless containing such things as tea and bi-carbonate of soda and cream-of-tartar. The men sat themselves on the sacks and biscuit tins while Padruig dragged clumsily at a

heap of rope fenders stored in a corner. Gallantly he handed
me a fender, assuring me that it would be a very comfortable
seat. There were still not enough seats so a long plank of
wood was brought in and supported on two cans of paraffin.

It was a full half hour later when Erchy and Niall arrived,
followed by Hector shepherding in the three Americans who
had been hesitant about following the rest of the crowd,
fearing they might not be welcome. But of course they were.

'Come away in, mo ghaoils,' invited Mairi, Padruig's wife,
in much the same tones she would have used if they had been
her neighbours for years. 'Come away in an' seat yourselves.'
It was easier said than done but room was made for two of
them on the plank. Hector, who had of course contrived to
occupy one of the chairs, indicated to the blond that she
should sit on his knee. She did so happily, amid light-hearted
warnings.

Mairi was already buttering scones while behind her a
girdle containing another batch was hanging above a fire of
driftwood piled high on the flat stone hearth. A steaming
kettle stood to one side.

'Will I fuse the tea?' asked Morag helpfully. Mairi with a
nod of her head directed her to the biscuit tin on which
Johnny was seated and she disturbed him to scoop out handfuls of tea into the large, smoke-blackened metal pot.

'An' how's bothyin' agreein' with you, Mairi?' enquired
Anna Vic.

'Ach, I like it fine,' replied Mairi. 'It makes like a holiday
for me.'

It is unusual to find a woman in residence in a watcher's
bothy. Normally the men fend for themselves while they are
watching, hence the sketchiness of the accommodation. However, when Mairi's husband, Padruig, and her son, Sandy,
had taken the job of watchers for the season, she, being a

conscientious wife and mother, had insisted on sharing their life at the bothy. She had also brought their one cow and their hens, maintaining that the change had made like a holiday' for them too.

One of the Americans was looking puzzled. She was tall, bespectacled and pimply and she had a loud, insistent voice.

'Don't you have any room but this one?' she asked.

Mairi admitted that this was their only accommodation.

'You mean the three of you share this room—even for sleeping?' asked the girl.

'There's not three of us sleepin 'at the same time,' Mairi told her. 'My husband and my son are here to watch, not to sleep.'

'What about the mails? Do you get any mails here?'

'Indeed yes!' There was more than a trace of indignation in Mairi's voice. 'Once or twice a week the man comes over. When there's anythin' worth bringin' to folk such as ourselves. We wouldn't expect him to come all this way with somethin' that didn't matter.'

'But what about supplies? How do you manage for food and things?'

'We brought them when we came.' Mairi nodded proudly towards the line of full sacks and tins. 'With that an' the milk we get from the cow an' eggs from my few hens. An' with the sea full of fish an' a salmon for the takin' why would we be needin' supplies?' Mairi was very patient. 'Are there no parts of your country, mo ghaoil, where they have river watchers that cannot get to the shops?'

The girl looked a little subdued. 'I guess so, but they wouldn't have to manage without a telephone nearby and electricity.'

'Aye,' said Mairi, 'I believe in your country they're great ones for the electric.'

'Where's Sandy away to?' asked Erchy.

'He's away collectin' gulls' eggs,' Padruig told him. He'll be back in a wee whiley I doubt.'

Erchy inclined his head in the direction of Ealasaid. 'I'm thinkin' you're right,' he said knowingly.

Ealasaid gave no indication that she had heard either question or reply and continued her chatter with her friends.

'Are you hearin' me?' Erchy called to her.

She gave him a pert glance. 'I'm hearin' you,' she replied with a toss of her head. The company exchanged winks and grins.

Ealasaid was the shepherd's daughter and she was extremely beautiful; tall and slim and creamy-complexioned with hair that glowed red as a heather fire on a dark night. All the men of the village paid tribute to her beauty but it was only Sandy who could make her blush. She was a kindly girl, gentle and yet always ready for fun, admirably suited one would have said for the career of nursing which she had chosen to follow. Unfortunately for Ealasaid, however, soon after commencing her training her mother had died and Ealasaid had thought it only right to come home and look after her father and the croft. She expressed no regret at having to forsake her career and I wondered sometimes if perhaps the necessary separation from Sandy it had entailed had worried her more than she cared to disclose. Even before leaving school Ealasaid and Sandy had become close friends and everyone predicted their eventual union. But Sandy it seemed was in no hurry to marry and now Ealasaid was receiving the ardent attention of a man from a neighbouring village who though comparatively rich was despised by the Bruachites.

Anna Vic passed round large mugs of steaming tea. There were only half a dozen mugs available so we shared, passing them to one another and sipping as we felt inclined. If we wanted a piece of scone we jumped up and helped ourselves from the dish on the table.

'Here's Sandy now,' announced Padruig. There came the sound of whistling and footsteps from outside. Ealasaid turned her back towards the door and Sandy came in, filling the doorway with his tallness and broadness. He was a splendid looking man, fair haired and with a face that would have struck one as grim except for the wrinkles at the corners of his eyes and a slight whimsical twist to the corners of his tight mouth. He was quiet and dour even among his friends and yet he was liked and admired by everyone. He reminded me of Gary Cooper and had I been twenty years younger I have no doubt I should have fallen head over heels in love with him myself.

In his hand Sandy carried a large milk pail full to the top with gulls' eggs. He put the pail on the table and nodded to his father. Padruig immediately took up the large iron cooking pot and went outside. He returned with it half full of water and into it the eggs were put, one by one, after being tested in a bowl of sea water—the good ones sank, the bad ones floated. Sandy hung the pot over the fire and half an hour later when they were hard boiled we were all peeling the shells off the eggs and biting into their goodness. The American girls were enthralled until one of them found an embryo in hers.

'It's all right,' Erchy assured her. 'You just pick that part out and throw it away.' But she threw the remains into the fire. 'You would need to have your gulls' eggs scrambled,' he advised her. 'You don't notice things like that then.'

'The tide's goin down pretty fast,' said Niall and stood up. 'We'd best be away.'

Hector decanted the blonde from his knee and jumped up.

'We'll away an' bring in the boat,' he said, going to the door.
Erchy and Niall followed him. 'We'll blow on the cow's horn
as soon as we're ready.' Ealasaid was the only one to show
signs of impatience.

'Ach, Ealasaid's wantin' plenty of time to get ready for
the big dance tomorrow,' said Anna Vic.

Sandy spoke. 'Dance? What dance?'

'Why, Ealasaid's fine fellow's givin' a dance tomorrow
night. He's hired a hall for it an' got the fiddler an' the
melodeon comin'. It's to be a grand do. Did you no hear?'

'An' Ealasaid's the only one from here invited,' supplied
one of the girls. 'He's only havin' his swanky friends apart
from her.'

'An' she has a new dress for it,' said Anna Vic.

Sandy looked straight at Ealasaid. 'You'll no be goin'.' It
was as much a statement as a question.

'Indeed I am so,' I noticed Ealasaid did not look at Sandy
as she spoke and they did not seek each other out when
goodbyes were being said.

Back at Bruach Morag and Anna Vic and I were in the
last dinghy load to go ashore and by the time we stepped
out the rest of the party had disappeared up the brae.

'Oidche Mhath!' we called to one another as we were
about to disperse.

'Here, wait a minute!' Erchy summoned. We turned to see
what was happening. 'We have somethin' for you,' he said.
'We managed to get the net across the river after all, while
we had the lend of Padruig's dinghy.'

Hector lifted the floor boards of the boat. Underneath lay
half a dozen fresh salmon.

The following evening Bruach had its own small excitement when an auction sale was held in the schoolroom, the
money raised being for an old people's home. The 'auction

sale' would be better described as a 'bring and buy' sale for
everyone had given what they could which meant that there
was a plethora of eggs and sacks of potatoes with perhaps a
dozen half-bottles and bottles of whisky. No-one therefore
wanted to buy eggs or potatoes but nevertheless bidding was
spirited and immediately they were knocked down to a
buyer they were put back into the sale. Even the whisky
had to go back in time after time until perhaps the eventual
buyer would have paid as much as seven pounds for a bottle.
At the end of the sale the whisky was quickly disposed of on
the spot and the eggs and potatoes—those that were left
after the children had quite literally 'had their fling'—were
packed up and put on the bus for delivery to the hospital.
We were preparing to put the schoolroom to rights and go
to our homes when Sandy appeared.

'You may as well shift the desks round the wall and clear
the floor ready for the dance,' he instructed us in his clipped
authoritative voice.

Everyone looked at him in surprise.

'We've no permission to have a dance here,' Janet told him.

'We have so,' returned Sandy shortly. No-one ever doubted
what Sandy said. Somehow, he had obtained permission for
a dance and his statement was accepted without further
questioning.

'But what about the music?' One of the young girls spoke
up. 'A dance is no good without a piper or a fiddler.'

'We have a fiddler an' a melodeon,' Sandy told her. 'Here
they are an' all ready to play.' He stood aside to allow two
tousle-headed men into the room. One was carrying a fiddle,
the other a melodeon.

'My God!' said Erchy, and his eyes were twinkling. 'Come
on, get these desks out of the way.' The floor was soon cleared,
the music began, but Sandy disappeared.

The story came out later.

Sandy, being determined that Ealasaid should not go dancing with her rich suitor, had taken the day off and gone to the village where lived the two musicians who had been engaged to play at the suitor's dance. There he had contrived some business with them, had treated them generously to whisky, delaying them until they missed the bus, and then suggested that as he was hiring a car to get him home they would be welcome to a lift. He would drop them off at the hall on the way home, he had assured them. The musicians were pathetically grateful but Sandy had told his driver to go slowly and before long the two men had been sleeping off their excesses in the back of the car. When they awoke they were in Bruach and as the hired car had returned immediately and there was no chance of their getting any other transport that evening, in Bruach they had to stay. In short, Sandy had kidnapped the band and as he had promised to pay the men the same fee as they had expected to receive from their official engagement they were happy enough to play for a Bruach dance.

When Sandy disappeared from the school, after seeing the dance commence satisfactorily, he went straight to Ealasaid's house and there he waited until she was brought home by her sulky suitor. As soon as the man had taken his leave Sandy confronted Ealasaid.

'Did you enjoy your dance?' he asked.

'There was no dance. There was no band arrived an' everybody sat around, not knowin' how to enjoy themselves.'

'Aye, that's the trouble with these swanky folks,' Sandy agreed. 'They've forgotten how to enjoy themselves while they're makin' money.'

'Dear knows what happened to the band,' said Ealasaid.

'They were nearly off their heads lookin' for them but nobody saw a sign of them.'

'Ach, they're down at the schoolhouse playin' for our dance,' Sandy told her. 'I've come to take you there now.'

'Here? In Bruach?' Ealasaid was at first horrified and then as Sandy explained she dissolved into laughter.

It was after midnight when the two of them arrived at the schoolhouse and immediately the pair rushed into a Schottische.

For the rest of the night, when Ealasaid wasn't dancing with Sandy she was sitting looking at him with wide adoring eyes. At the end of the season of watching the pair slipped quietly off to Glasgow and were married.

A Vest for St. Peter

JOHNNY and Erchy were entertaining an obviously appreciative cluster of friends outside the door of the byre on Erchy's croft. I called a greeting as I passed on my way to the Post Office and was summoned to join them.

'Here, look at this!' commanded Erchy pulling off his gumboot to expose a thick sock that had been darned with so many bright colours it looked like a child's attempt at tapestry. There was a renewed outburst of shrieks and sniggers from the group. I too found myself smiling broadly.

'I can guess who's responsible for that,' I said.

'Aye, indeed,' replied Erchy feelingly. 'I only put it on just for a bit of a laugh. My mother was for puttin' the lot at the back of the fire when she saw them.'

'It's partly my fault, I suppose,' I confessed.

'You? Was it you put her up to it?'

'No, but I happened to drop in at her cottage when she was darning your socks. She'd just finished the first one and when I saw she'd used bright green wool for the toe and orange for the heel I couldn't help a bit of a chuckle.'

'That would do it,' Erchy accused. 'She's a right queer one for wantin' to get a laugh.' He put on his boot. 'They were no bad socks till she got a hold of them,' he complained. 'Now I'll need to get new ones from the tinks when they come.'

'She was after my mother to give her some of mine for darnin',' put in Johnny.

'Did she get them?'

'Aye. I'll need to try an' get them from her before she spoils them.'

'You'll be too late,' I told him. 'She prides herself on being a fast worker.'

'They'll go under the kettle if she does what she's after doin' with Erchy's,' he threatened. 'She must be thinkin' we're like the tinkers ourselves to be wantin' colours like that on our feets.' He hammered a wooden tooth into his hayrake.

'Did you see the socks she knitted for the Children's Home?' I enquired.

'Aye, I did,' replied Johnny. 'An' I feel sorry for the poor childrens.'

The Home had advertised for voluntary knitters, offering

to supply wool to anyone who would knit socks for the children. Miss Parry, Bruach's newest resident, had immediately responded and soon a large parcel of wool had arrived—enough to knit a dozen or so pairs of socks, each pair to be a different colour. A few days later when Morag and I had called at Miss Parry's house we found she had already knitted up most of the wool and the finished socks were laid out in what were supposed to be pairs. Morag and I had exchanged secret glances. The socks were merely long tubes joined together at the toe and out of the twenty odd socks it was impossible to pick out two that were identical in size and colour. I forced a smile, to which Miss Parry responded with a delighted giggle.

'I'm hoping they'll get a good laugh when they see them,' she simpered behind her spectacles. 'And orphans need a bit of a laugh.'

Morag picked up a sock and examined it. 'Did they no ask you to turn the heel?' she asked guilelessly.

There was a moment of tight silence before Miss Parry acknowledged the question and when she spoke her voice was harsh and the twinkle in her eyes had been switched off.

'Orphans don't need heels,' she snapped.

Miss Parry had come to the village of Bruach about six months previously, having taken over the cottage once occupied by the two spinsters who had been known locally as the 'lady pilgrims'.* She was a tall, bony woman who Erchy described as 'lookin' as if she was made out of knittin' needles' and lived a life of austerity that astonished even the Bruachites. Her cottage was the traditional 'but an' ben,' that is, two rooms, one a kitchen and the other a bedroom with a tiny cupboard of a larder interposed between them. Her kitchen was bleak and sparsely furnished with two

* See 'The Sea for Breakfast'.

bentwood chairs, a small sewing table which also served as a
dining table, a sewing machine and two large black chests
on one of which reposed a tiny lamp that gave no more
illumination than a candle. The firegrate was always empty
because Miss Parry 'couldn't stand heat' and the only warmth
came from a tiny oilstove which also supported a kettle,
though so suspicious was she of oilstoves that the flame was
never more than a thin rim of blue and the kettle rarely
managed anything above a sigh of frustration. There were
no curtains or blinds but she kept sheets of brown paper to
pin over the windows at night or when the sun should have
the temerity to peep in at her.

It was impossible to completely list her innumerable 'hates'
but the sun and children ranked high among them. She also
hated animals because they smelled or they might trip her
up; she hated flowers because they reminded her of death;
she hated birds because they were too noisy. And yet despite
her aversions she was generally a smiling, seemingly good
natured woman who enjoyed nothing better than bestowing
gifts on her neighbours. It was a pity that her neighbours
could not share her enjoyment but the trouble was that Miss
Parry's gifts were mostly unusable or unwearable. She would
knit pullovers for the men but so determined was she to
impress people with the speed and economy of her knitting
that after the welt and a few inches of pattern she would
begin to cast off for the sleeves and neck. Consequently the
recipients found that if they lifted their arms the welt would
rise up and threaten to choke them. I have never seen men's
faces express such pathetic dejection as when they first tried
on one of Miss Parry's hand knitted pullovers. Yet, even
when they were tried on in her presence Miss Parry could see
no fault in her workmanship and I think she never even
bothered to suspect that the women had to unpick all the

garments and re-knit them before they could be worn.

The more intimately I got to know her the more her way
of life astonished me. She wasted nothing and seemed
content to spend all her time sitting in her cheerless kitchen
devising uses for odd pieces of material and lengths of wool
of which she must have kept a prodigious store. If she heard
of any one being ill she would soon have knitted them an
unwearable bed jacket or, if it was a man, it would be a
pair of bedsocks that were comparable in size to a baby's
bootees. When someone complained in her hearing that
they could not buy some article of clothing from the mail
order store Miss Parry would set to work and contrive an
alternative. She once heard me lamenting that it was
difficult to get comfortable bras when one had to depend for
choice on a mail order catalogue. Within a few days she was
at my cottage with half a dozen bras, designed and made
especially for me from odd pieces of material out of her
ragbag. I was horrified. One bra was made of Harris tweed,
another in Buchanan tartan, yet another in stiff calico. The
rest were in an assortment of sad cottons and they had all
been achieved by sewing together two large triangles of
material that looked more like boat sails than lingerie. The
triangles were bound with broad black tape, lengths of which
had been left for tying the garment around me.

'They'll last you longer than anything you could buy from
a shop,' she predicted happily—and truthfully. I managed
to comment favourably on them and restrained my laughter
until I could try on a 'bra' in the privacy of my own bedroom.
Even when I pulled the tapes to their limit the boat sails
came underneath my armpits and the shoulder straps fell
in loops down my back. Miss Parry had once confided to
me that both her own breasts had been removed because
of cancer and I was forced to the conclusion that it must have

been such a long time ago that she had forgotten the usual location of such female appurtenances.

The Bruachites soon grew to think of Miss Parry as a professional invalid. She looked well but she boasted of having had so many operations that her life must have been lived in and out of hospitals. Besides having had both her breasts removed she informed me at various times that she had lost her womb; her gall bladder and one kidney; her appendix had been removed in a station waiting room because the train that should have taken her to the hospital had got snowed up; she suffered from high blood pressure and had at different times broken both her arms and both her ankles. In fact one got the impression that so often had she been at death's door she had wedged a decisive foot there to keep it open. Considering everything she was remarkably strong, as I found to my cost when I once gave her a supporting arm on the way back to her cottage. She was a quick and clumsy walker and had stumbled so often that the frequent tugs on my arm had left me feeling as limp as if I had done a strenuous day's work.

The most puzzling thing about Miss Parry was her diet. No-one ever saw her cooking or partaking of a meal in her own house and the grocer reported that she bought no more from him than would have kept a mouse alive. The first time I had invited her to a meal had been on Sunday evening after church. The table was set with my home-made bread and butter, a cheese soufflé and scones and cake. To me it all looked very appetising but Miss Parry declined everything save a half slice of bread which she asked if she might have toasted. It was barely warm before she indicated that it was done sufficiently and she refused butter with it—butter 'vexed her insides', she said. When I started to pour out tea she stopped me before the cup was half full and requested

that it should be topped up with cold water. She took no
sugar or milk. While she nibbled at her wan toast and sipped
at pallid tea I tried not to feel too uncomfortable as I tucked
into cheese soufflé. Religion always makes me hungry and
as I had taken a good deal of trouble with the meal I was
not going to see it wasted.

'Are you sure you've had enough?' I asked her anxiously
when I considered we had sat long enough at the table.

'Plenty,' she replied in a Sabbath whisper. 'I never eat
more than that.'

I wondered if she suffered still with her stomach. She was
quick to tell me she had ulcers.

While we washed and dried the dishes she told me the story
of her life. Her parents had died when she was small and she
and her young brother had been brought up by their grand-
parents, characters so harsh they could have come from the
pages of a Cronin novel. Life had been hard; comfort
condemned as smacking of the devil and his works. Every
morning after a breakfast of porridge and milk, brother and
sister, carrying a thick slice of plain bread for their lunch
'piece', had walked the six miles to school each day. Returning home they would be given work to do on the croft or in
the house. There were no near neighbours and the children
were allowed no friends to visit them. On Saturday nights they
were given a bath in a doorless shed beside the house and
winter and summer a bucket of cold water was emptied over
them to 'toughen them'. This was followed by a dose of
laxative from granny to rid them of the week's poisons and
a thrashing from their grandfather to rid them of the week's
sins. They would then be sent to bed with no candles to
light them up to the dark bedrooms and no hot water bottles
to warm the chill sheets though the windows were nailed
wide open all the year round. When she had left school Miss

Parry had trained as a teacher and had continued to teach until her retirement five years previously. She had never made close friends with anyone; never had a boy-friend or even thought of the possibility of a boy-friend. The only leavening in her life had been her church-going and her frequent visits to hospital. I wondered why she had come to Bruach. 'I always wanted adventure,' she said.

When Miss Parry returned my hospitality I made certain I ate a substantial meal before I went. And of course I found she had provided amply. There was tinned meat and tinned fruit and shop bread and shortbread and the tea was so strong I could have danced on it as it came out of the pot. I wilted before the sight of it but I had to endure.

'I know you have a good appetite,' said Miss Parry, twinkling, and pushed all the meat and bread at me, except for the one half slice she ate herself.

Next time I was in the grocer's he said: 'I hear you went for a meal with Miss Parry one day last week?'

I admitted I had.

'I was wonderin' why she suddenly bought all that food,' he told me, giving me a look of great respect.

There were times when Bruach wondered a good deal about Miss Parry. Did she have any living relatives and if she had why didn't she go to see them. Everyone was greatly interested therefore when she announced that her brother and his wife were to pay her a visit. They arrived one perfect day of August; a day of high skies and sun with a breeze soft as a silk shawl teasing the bay into iridescent ripples and filling the air with the scent of new-mown hay. I was invited to tea to meet them and when I arrived I was astonished to see the small sewing table and the two wooden chairs outside in the neglected garden.

'It's a pity to waste all this sunshine,' said Miss Parry's sister-in-law as she busied herself carrying out plates and cups and saucers. 'Come and sit down,' she bade me. Her husband appeared with a wooden box and a stool. We sat waiting for Miss Parry.

'Is Miss Parry coming to sit outside?' I enquired timidly, thinking of her determination to avoid sunshine on her person or in her house.

'I've told her she must. It will do her good,' said her sister-in-law and raised her voice in summons.

Miss Parry came outside, trying unsuccessfully to conceal her glowering looks beneath twitching, tight-lipped smiles. She sat rigidly in her chair, refusing to eat even her meagre half slice of toast. As soon as her brother and his wife had departed she took to her bed. The sun had made her ill, she maintained.

For some time after their visit Miss Parry received parcels of books from her brother who, it seemed, had been dismayed by the drabness of his sister's life. She read them and then passed them on to me to keep. She did not like having books about the house, they looked untidy. Sometimes she commented on them and once when I found a copy of a somewhat suggestive book among the bundle she had brought me I asked her if she had read it.

'Yes, I did,' she said.

'Did you enjoy it?'

'I enjoyed some of it,' she admitted. 'Did you?'

'I did,' I acknowledged, 'but I'm a little surprised at you. Some of the passages I should have expected you to condemn.'

'Oh, those,' she retorted, 'I just took my glasses off when I came to them.'

She continued her lonely and industrious life in Bruach for close on two years before we noticed disturbing signs of odd behaviour. She imagined she was receiving poison-pen letters though she refused to quote the contents and could never show any evidence of such missives. Her suspicions centred on Do-do, her nearest neighbour on whose croft her cottage was situated. Originally Do-do's offence had been that when Miss Parry had bestowed upon him one of her notorious pullovers Do-do had tried it on in front of her and had openly mocked and derided its shape. Thereafter she had refused to speak to him and whenever his name was mentioned her eyes had grown dark and brooding. She accused him of tormenting her by hanging round her cottage after dark and making strange noises. The Bruachites refused to believe for one instant that there was any substance in her complaints though it was not long before one or two of the more heartless ones had seen to it that there were strange noises near her cottage at night. The next thing we heard was that she was complaining of Do-do's lack of hygiene. He was making appalling smells, she claimed, and pointed out that though he was old and rheumaticky and could not get out to the moors to relieve his bowels there was no 'wee hoosie' on his croft. How then did he manage? Miss Parry had soon convinced herself that he was using the vicinity of her house, hence the smells. At last Erchy resolved to put the question to Do-do and let the old man defend himself. He reported at the next ceilidh.

' "Do-do," I says to him. "How do you manage about gettin' to the moors now your rheumatisn is so bad?"

' "I don't manage," says he.

' "Well you have no wee hoosie," says I, "so what do you do about it?"

' "Well, Erchy," he says: "You know me well enough, an' you know I'm never without a good fire. When I feel the need I spread a piece of paper on the hearth an' when I'm finished it's straight into the fire with it. What can be more hygienic than that?" he asked me.'

I was in hospital when Miss Parry became ill though before she was herself taken away she had time to send me a voluminous garment which she described as her own design of dressing gown. It was merely a length of very wide material folded in half and a hole cut in the top. The side seams had been left open to make armholes somewhere in the region of my waist. I tried it on for the entertainment of my fellow patients and wondered how Miss Parry's eyes would have reacted to their laughter.

A few days after I had returned home from hospital I received a letter from Miss Parry's brother telling me that his wife was coming to the cottage to dispose of his sister's furniture as she would not be returning. The sister-in-law called to see me.

'She says that you must have the chest she's marked and its contents,' she told me. 'And if there's anything else you've a fancy for, for Goodness's sake take that and save me the bother of having to get rid of it,' she added.

Together we examined the chest, which had a little label stuck on to it with the words 'For Miss Beckwith'. We lifted the lid. It contained:

One roll of cotton-wool,
One roll cellulose wadding,
Dozens of bandages of various widths,
A stomach pump,
An enema,
A bed pan,
Three feeding bottles,
Two vomit bowls,
Six draw sheets,
Two invalid cups.

Rooting right at the bottom we also found a stirrup-pump. We stood gazing at each other in mute bewilderment.

'Whatever did she use that for?' asked the sister-in-law. My own thoughts were, 'What did she expect me to use it for?'

We tackled the other chest, reeling from the smell of camphor, and when we had excavated all the oddments of material and bundles of wool we found a boldly labelled dress-box. The label said, 'My laying out clothes for when I die'. Once again we exchanged glances. The sister-in-law carefully lifted the lid. The garments inside were made in fine white cotton and neatly folded; tucked inside them was another parcel. Cautiously the sister-in-law extracted it. It was something wrapped in many layers of tissue paper.

'Whatever's this?' Her tones were awestruck. She finished unwrapping it and displayed a strange-looking garment knitted in white wool. A label sewn to its hem proclaimed it to be 'A vest for St. Peter'.

'St. Peter!' gasped the sister-in-law. 'And her a good presbyterian all her life.'

I asked that my regards should be conveyed to Miss Parry along with the hope that she would soon be better.

'She's not likely to get better,' the sister-in-law confided. 'The doctor's told us that.'

'Poor soul,' I said.

'If only she would settle in hospital she'd stand more chance of lasting a bit longer,' she said, 'but she hates it there. Of course,' she added, 'when you've been strong and healthy all your life it must be dreadful to have to face a long spell in hospital.'

'But I thought she'd spent a lot of time in hospital,' I exclaimed.

'Not her,' said her sister-in-law. 'Never a day's illness in her life until now, the lucky woman.'

'No Ortinary . . .'

ON winter evenings in Bruach there was always a ceilidh taking place in someone's house. A 'ceilidh' could be only two people—one neighbour dropping in on another for a 'wee crack' as it was called, but a real ceilidh needed at least a dozen people so that there was more likelihood of a too serious conversation being interrupted with song or a too

vehement argument being quelled by laughter. Every village
had its favourite ceilidh house: places of which it could be
said 'There's aye good ceilidhin' there'. Usually the houses
had achieved this distinction by having had at some time
among it's occupants a good 'seanachaidh' or story-teller who
could draw the people to hear his tales. In Bruach Janet's
house was easily the favourite venue. There was no
'seanachaidh' residing there now but in the days when
Janet's home had been one of the old 'black houses' as they
are known in the Hebrides, where the fire sat on a stone
hearth in the centre of the earth floor and a barrel hung
below a hole in the thatched roof to help coax out the lazy
smoke, there had lived an uncle of hers who had been considered a great storyteller. The crofters had come regularly
to ceilidh and to listen to the old man and though he had been
dead for forty years and Janet now lived in a much more
sophisticated house with a corrugated iron roof, linoleum
covered floors and a polished range that hurried its smoke
into a conventional chimney, the aura of the old ceilidh house
and its 'seanachaidh' still clung. There were men in the
village who would not have thought an evening complete
without at least twenty minutes of it being spent at Janet's
fireside. There they would sit, borrowing her brother's
spectacles to read his newspaper, and afterwards criticising
his croft and his cattle; mocking at his lack of skill with a
gun and arguing his right to some coveted piece of driftwood,
while all the time helping themselves from his jar of baking
soda to relieve their indigestion.

Wherever they could be sure of two or three people being
gathered together there would the rest of the Bruachites feel
impelled to congregate and so one would expect to find the
largest, most animated ceilidhs taking place in Janet's
lamplit, wood walled kitchen.

It was tacitly understood by everyone that ceilidhing did not begin until after the evening chores were over, so the earliest callers did not appear until round about seven o'clock. From that hour on sporadic thumpings of gumbooted feet in the porch served not only to announce new arrivals but also to reduce the quantity of mud they might otherwise have carried into the kitchen on their boots. Except for tourists in the summer no-one ever thought of knocking on a Bruach door. If a knock had been heard on a winter evening it would certainly have been ignored since the assumption would have been that some of the lads of the village were playing a joke. Save at Halloween such behaviour was rare but the possibility that it might be a stranger's knock would not immediately have occurred to anyone because strangers on a winter evening were even rarer.

At Janet's ceilidhing was so much a part of normal everyday life that no Bruachite was likely to be invited to 'Come away in' after the preliminary thuds. They just opened the door, gently if they were inclined to be shy, thrustingly if they were pretending they were not shy; glanced quickly around to see who had already arrived, and then slid into the nearest available space whether it was a seat on the wooden bench or a vacant patch on the floor. Only if you were an outsider like myself would it be likely for you to receive a nod of welcome or recognition but by their very indifference the crofters would become immediately integrated into the gathering, absorbed in its atmosphere of hospitality and friendliness.

The true, spontaneous Highland ceilidhs are a wonderful institution; the complete antidote to loneliness. No-one is ever unwelcome and old or young you may come and go as you please. You may contribute to the discussion or you may sit quietly and listen; you may pose an inflammatory question and then sit back and let other more passionate contenders pursue it to an irate, or more often amusing, conclusion; you might hum a snatch of song and be leading a lusty chorus after only a bar or two; you could claim to have seen a ghost (a 'wee mannie' was the most generally acceptable) and at once have the ears and eyes of the company concentrated on you, avid not only to hear your story but to be awed by it.

Ceilidhs varied according to the company or to the news or to the weather. If there was a preponderance of old men reminiscence would almost certainly dominate the evening's conversation. When Hector or Erchy was present talk about the sea and boats was inevitable, and the militant Tearlaich —described by Morag as 'Him that would make a quarrel in an empty house'—had only to have his broad, hunched shoulders half way through the door before he had provoked everyone to argument. Tearlaich's capacity for dispute was impressive. The Bruachites related in shocked tones how once he and his mate had taken some tourists on a boat trip to one of the outlying Islands. When the time had come for their return and the boat had loaded her passengers a fierce argument had erupted between the two men. The boat lurched and wallowed as the argument grew more vehement and the passengers sat in a terrified silence, unable to understand a word of the crackle and hiss of vituperative Gaelic. Suddenly a man who had not been one of the original party appeared scrambling quickly over the rocks towards the boat. He shouted to the boat men to help him get aboard but, ignoring him they continued upbraiding each other and left him to struggle aboard alone. As soon as his foot touched the deck the man lay down. It was minutes later that one of the party of tourists managed to raise his voice sufficiently to quell the protagonists. 'Are you aware that you have a

corpse aboard this boat?' he shouted at them and having
thus commanded their attention he indicated the prostrate
figure. Undoubtedly the man was dead.

When I made up my mind to go to a ceilidh I always
hoped that certain people would be there, my favourite being
Fiona. Fiona was a dear kind old soul; lumpish in shape, tattily
clad and always reeking of staleness. Though I recoiled from
close proximity to her I enjoyed her company, cherishing her
presence in much the same way I cherished the presence of
the compost heap at the bottom of the garden—regretful
of its appearance and odour but grateful for the bountiful
goodness that was constantly working away inside. Given the
chance Fiona would have taken upon herself the troubles
and toils of the whole village. She was available if anyone
needed a temporary nurse for an old relative or a sick cow;
she was ready to lend a hand at the making of haggis and
black pudding whenever a sheep was killed; she would lay out
a corpse or pluck a hen and if someone ran short of bread
she was so good-hearted she would give them her last half
loaf. I have even seen her take the sweet from her mouth to
give to a child. Although she had never been off the island
Fiona was by no means lacking in shrewdness and guile.
She was however at times confounded by modern acquisi-
tions which most of the Bruachites had by now come to
accept. She would not go near a telephone for instance and
water running from a tap, when she had a chance of seeing
such a thing, was still a source of great delight. A camera was
an inexplicable machine and a photograph something to be
exclaimed over as much for its existence as for its subject
matter. She had been at my house one evening when I was
giving a show of colour slides, most of which I had taken
myself in and around the village. Fiona had sat very quietly
indeed until I put a slide into the projector which showed the

cottage where Angus, the fisherman, lived with his mother.
It was an excellent photograph, so clear that it showed the
dribble of tar over one window and the unlit lamp on the
sill inside. Around the wide open door was grouped an
expectant cluster of hens, obviously anticipating a feed, and
the quality of the photograph was such that one found one-
self awaiting the appearance of Angus's mother at the door
with a bowl of mash. Amid appreciative murmurs of
identification and approval Fiona suddenly jumped up.

'I must away an' shut that door!' she explained in answer
to our enquiries. 'There's Angus away to the sea this very
mornin' an' his mother away in Glasgow an' there's the door
wide open. Yon hens will take every bit of food in the house
if I don't close it.'

The presence of Fiona at a ceilidh invariably evoked tales
of the supernatural, for she was unashamedly greedy for old
legends and stories of mystery. There needed only to be the
tiniest whisper of a slightly out of the ordinary happening
and instantly Fiona would attach to it magical associations
and would launch into one of her numerous tales of strange
predictions and stranger events. When her story ended someone else would be exhorted to contribute a tale and so it
would continue for the rest of the evening. There is no doubt
in my mind that tales of the supernatural were accepted by
the Bruachites as being factual. And indeed I found it
difficult to be sceptical when I was listening to such unequi-
vocal narration in an ambience of lamplight and peatsmoke;
listening to old men who could preface their stories with 'I
mind when I was a wee lad my grandfather tellin' me' . . .;
listening to people who could tell of first-hand encounters
with ghosts or wee folk which might be recollections of
thirty years ago or might be an experience of the previous
week. One had to be a cynic to discount stories told with such

conviction. It was not so easy to be cynical when after a
night of such cosy mystery you had to walk home across
lonely moors where the wind hummed eerily in the corries;
malign shadows dogged your path, and there were sudden
and inexplicable cold breaths over your shoulders. Even in
daylight there were parts of the moor which were too oppres-
sive for anyone to wish to be there alone. In the dark one
hardly dared to look in their direction.

One clear fine night in October I was sitting in my own
kitchen with my ear pushed almost inside an ebbing radio
set trying to pick up the essential clues in a tensely exciting
murder mystery. Just when the final denouement was about
to be made however the radio gave a final whimper and died
completely. I swore at it; I twiddled knobs, and shook it
without being rewarded with so much as a scratch of atmos-
pherics. Disgusted, I turned away from it and at that moment
there came a growl of wind in the chimney and the kitchen
was filled with smoke. Every chimney in Bruach suffered at
some time or another from wind blowing down it but for-
tunately it was not always the same wind direction that
affected all the chimneys. I knew that Janet's chimney never
misbehaved itself at the same time as mine so I resolved to
go and join the inevitable ceilidh around her fire. I slung a
coat over my shoulders and held it together with my left
hand, my right hand being bandaged and in a sling since I
had fallen on it two weeks previously. I opened the door into
Janet's kitchen and she looked up in surprise. Her face broke
into a welcoming smile as she urged someone to make room
for me near the fire. This much of a stranger I knew I should
always be in Bruach.

'An' how's your poor, dear wrist, Miss Peckwitt?' It was
Fiona's anxious voice and I turned happily to acknowledge
her and her enquiry. Anything that was ailing was always

poor and dear to Fiona. You might hear her say one time, 'The poor, dear man has gone to his rest,' and another time she might be bemoaning, 'The poor, dear bus has a hole in its wheel.'

I told her that my wrist didn't seem to be getting much better. It was still very painful.

'I'm sayin' I wouldn't be surprised if you've broken it,' Erchy chipped in through the general commiseration.

'I suspected that myself,' I admitted, 'but the doctor has X-rayed it and he's quite confident there's nothing broken.'

'Ach, him! I doubt but he'd have X-rayed it through the bottom of a whisky bottle,' commented Morag and looked round the gathering for their appreciation.

' 'Tis wonderful indeed these X-rays,' asserted Fiona. 'They tell me they can look right through your bones with them.'

'Aye,' someone affirmed. 'They're clever, right enough, these days with their inventions.'

'Not so clever as in the old days,' objected Fiona. 'There was folks then that could look through the years without any machines to help them an' they'd tell us what was goin' to happen. I'm thinkin' it must be a lot easier to look through bones.'

'That reminds me,' I began, 'has anyone here ever had a pet raven or had any experience of a raven behaving in a very peculiar way?'

Their eyes were fixed on me. 'No, why do you ask?' they demanded and I told them of how that very afternoon I had gone for a long walk over the moors and that when I had reached a certain valley I had suddenly become aware of a raven which kept alighting a few yards in front of me and then rising to circle just above my head. Each time it had alighted it had croaked at me in such a familiar way that I

thought it must have at some time been a tame one. I tried to
return its croaking. When I had decided I had gone far
enough I turned towards home but then the raven had
seemed to become agitated and had flown several times in
front of my face as if trying to get me to turn back. Being
something of an amateur ornithologist I was intrigued by the
behaviour of the bird and did turn back. Once again the
raven resumed its antics, alighting a few paces in front of me
and croaking. It was so persistent that I got the impression
it wanted me to follow it and this I did for perhaps another
quarter of an hour. However tiredness overcame curiosity;
the bird seemed to be leading me on interminably and when
I thought of all the work that was awaiting me at home I
finally gave up the chase and turned in my tracks. Several
times the raven flew across my path as if trying to divert me
but ignoring it I kept steadily on. After a little while it
alighted on a projection of rock, croaked at me three or four
times with the air of a disgruntled hawker and watched me
disappear over the brow of the hill.

It struck me as strange that though down in the quiet
valley I had found the behaviour of the bird interesting and
rather endearing the moment I gained the brow of the hill
which looked down on to the familiar houses and crofts I
started to think of the incident as being a little uncanny and
began to wonder what they would make of it at the ceilidhs
when I told my story. I thought that the most likely explanation would be that someone had once caught and tamed the
bird and that it had since escaped or been allowed its freedom. But no-one knew of anyone who had at any time had a
pet raven, neither in Bruach nor anywhere else on the
island.

'You should have followed it,' Johnny suggested. 'It might
have led you to some treasure. Some of these beasts are

supposed to know where there's treasure an' if they take a fancy to you they'll lead you to it.'

'Indeed she was wise not to follow it any further than she did, I'm thinkin',' Anna Vic shuddered and gathered herself into her chair.

'What do you think was the reason for it then?' Erchy asked.

I shook my head. 'I can't think of anything unless it had a wounded mate or something like that. If it had been in the spring I'd have thought it might be trying to distract my attention from its nest or a young one but that's not likely at this time of year.'

Fiona said profoundly: 'I'm thinkin' it was no ordinary raven.'

As soon as she had spoken the atmosphere of the ceilidh was laced with tension; everyone waited expectantly, knowing, as I knew, what would ensue. How often had I heard a rich Highland voice prefacing a narrative with the carefully enunciated words: 'It was no ortinary . . .' The phrase was intended to convey that the 'no ortinary' animal was really a witch who had temporarily assumed that disguise for some specific purpose.

'Never follow that bird again should you see it,' Fiona enjoined me.

'But Johnny thinks it might have led me to some treasure,' I retorted, counteracting the solemnity that had settled on the gathering with an attempt at flippancy.

'Johnny knows fine it is not to treasure it would be after takin' you, but to some place . . .' She looked up at me and sensing my scepticism she faltered: '. . . to some place you might not wish to see,' she ended self-consciously.

'An' what might have happened to you then the dear only knows,' Anna Vic was quick to reinforce Fiona's warning.

'There's folks that's not been the same since they followed some gey queer animal or other.'

'Aye, aye,' there were varied murmurs of confirmation. I already knew the story of the men who had played with the Fairies and their subsequent fate. I knew too of the lucky escape of Erchy's uncle after he had once been foolish enough to follow an otter that 'wass no ortinary otter.' There were many such stories and nearly everyone in Bruach appeared to know of a relative of theirs who had been involved in some mysterious adventure.

'What might have happened to you we can only guess,' Fiona resumed now with a surge of confidence. 'Did you no hear, Miss Peckwitt, of the man that met the cat while he was ridin' back to his croft one night?'

'No,' I lied. I had more than once heard the story but not hitherto from Fiona and experience had taught me that the tales varied according to the narrator.

'Then you should know of it.' Fiona's grey eyes stared into the fire and the palms of her work-ravaged hands moved incessantly backwards and forwards over her skirt as she told the story of the local girl who had been jilted by her lover when it was proved to him that the girl's mother was an indisputable witch and that the daughter would surely become a witch herself. A few weeks after the jilting the lover was riding home one night just before dark when as he was approaching a narrow rocky pass he noticed a large black cat running in front of his horse. He tried to rein the horse away from it but the animal refused to obey and carried on into the pass. Here the cat suddenly turned and leapt at the horse, frightening it so that the man had almost been thrown. He had lashed at the cat with his whip but it had easily evaded him. The following night approaching the same spot the same thing happened but this time the cat succeeded in clawing the neck of the horse. The man was quite sure that on this occasion his whip had found its target but the cat made no sound of distress and he concluded that once again he had misjudged his stroke. He became so much troubled by these incidents that he had taken his story to the local seer, a seventh son of a seventh son, who was himself possessed of strange powers. The seer had at once identified the cat as being 'no ortinary cat' but in fact the jilted sweetheart who, being the daughter of a witch, had been able to assume this disguise in order to wreak revenge on her ex-lover. 'First she has lured your horse and frightened it; next she has clawed your horse, the third time it will be yourself she will be seeking to injure.' The seer then advised the man to carry a gun with him when he was riding home at night and to be sure to load the gun with a silver bullet—it was only silver that was effective against witches. He further cautioned him not to shoot to kill but only to wound and that immediately he had fired the gun he must gallop his horse straight for the house of the doctor and tell him everything that had happened. The man promised to do all this and before he again ventured to ride home in the dark he made a silver bullet from a six-pence and loaded it into his gun. Arrived at the place where the cat had attacked on the two previous occasions he held his gun in readiness. Sure enough there was the cat and this time when it leaped it was indeed into the man's flesh that its claws dug deep. He fired the gun and saw that he had succeeded in wounding the cat high in the right hindleg. He spurred his horse and raced for the doctor's house. The doctor, who was of course a son of the croft, listened attentively to the story and decided that they should get the local policeman to accompany them to the house of the witch. The policeman had knocked on the door and demanded entry several times before it was unbarred and opened by the old woman.

'We wish to have speech with your daughter,' he told her.

'My daughter is not well,' replied the old woman. 'She is in her bed.'

The doctor then stepped forward. 'If she is not well then I am here to cure her,' he asserted and pushing his way into the room he stood beside the recess bed where, sure enough, they found the ex-sweetheart. When the doctor drew back the clothes to examine the girl they saw the wound—which was just like a bullet wound—in her right thigh.

Fiona finished telling her story and there were a few seconds of silence before the shuffling of feet, the sniffings and spittings and the changing of positions began. Janet threw a couple of peats on to the fire and turned down the lamp which had begun to smoke.

'It was a strange thing the way that old witch could work,' said Hamish meditatively. 'I mind my grandfather was the only one hereabouts that she couldn't put a spell on.' He looked around for confirmation. 'She said so herself,' he added.

'Aye, that's right enough. Your grandfather was never afraid of the woman, I mind that,' affirmed old Roddy, 'Though I was never able to understand why.'

'I know why,' announced Hamish mysteriously.

Everyone looked at him. 'You do?'

'Aye, He told my father an' my father told me how he was able to manage it.' He fished in his pocket for a cigarette, lit it, took one long puff and then nipped it out and replaced it in the packet. The grocer had run out of cigarettes and everyone was having to economise. The complete silence and attention encouraged him to go on with his story.

'It was like this,' he told us. 'Every mornin' my grandfather

would read the bible for the family an' give hay to the cow
before he finished lacin' up his boots. Not until he had done
those two things would he pull up the laces an' tie the knot.
In the evenin' it was the other way; then he'd see to the cow
first, an' read the bible before he'd undo his laces. He never
forgot to do it this way an' he never breathed a word to a
soul that this was how he protected himself from the witch's
spells. Not until she was dead an' he told my father did he
mention it. But she knew all the same. He got a right scare
when she said to him one day, "There'll come a time,
Hamish Mor, when you'll forget about the lacings on your
boots an' then will be my chance." '

'If he never spoke to anybody of the way he saved himself
from her spells how did the witch come to know of it?' asked
Janet.

Hamish turned on her. 'That's just it, now. How would
she know unless she was a witch and had been tryin' to harm
him?'

'Was she never in his house?'

'Indeed, no.' The denials came in a chorus from the older
folk who remembered Hamish's grandfather. 'Your grandfather would as soon let in the devil himself as that woman.'

'She was a witch all right,' Hamish asserted.

'I'm damty sure she was,' corroborated Erchy.

It was at another ceilidh held in Janet's house that I heard
Fiona again tell the story of the cat and the witch. This time
the ceilidh had been an organized one in honour of a guest
of Janet's who was anxious to collect stories of the islands.
He was an earnest young man wearing spectacles that Morag
said were 'like the bottoms of glass bottles' and he sat with
his legs crossed and a note pad on his bony knees. I do not
know if he was too engrossed in the stories he heard to
remember his note pad or whether it was there merely to

impress the spectators but so far as I could see he made no single jotting during the whole evening.

When Fiona finished narrating the young man asked: 'Surely it couldn't have been a policeman they were supposed to have gone to? After all, policemen haven't been policemen for all that length of time.'

'Since my time an' before,' contradicted old Roddy indignantly.

'Yes, but surely this story must go back a lot longer than you or your immediate forbears?'

'Indeed no!' argued Roddy. 'How can that be when the witch is alive herself to this day?'

The young man managed to catch his pad as it slid off his knee. 'Alive today?' he repeated.

'Aye.' Roddy was firm. 'You mind it's not the old mother but the daughter that's alive an' she's well, though she's near ninety, I doubt.'

The young man had a very prominent Adam's apple and it travelled up and down several times before he spoke again.

'Where does she live?' he asked weakly.

Roddy told him. 'She's walked with a stick ever since . . .' Roddy recollected himself, 'ever since the accident to her leg,' he continued, 'an' she doesn't pretend to be a witch any more but she's alive today an' that's as true as I'm here.'

'An' she still has the wound in her right thigh, plain as I don't know what,' put in Hamish.

The young man looked no longer incredulous but eager.

'Would I be able to see her?' he asked.

'Surely,' they told him.

The next day the young man said good-bye to Janet and continued on his travels. The bus driver reported that he was asking more questions about the witch and had expressed his intention of loitering around her croft. The driver had suggested that he call on the old lady. She was, he assured the young man, quite harmless now and willing to admit she had once been a witch.

The last news we had of the young man was that he was in hospital. He had fallen somewhere, quite near the witch's croft it was said, and had injured his shoulder.

I could not help wondering if his injuries were the result of his going up to a strange woman and asking her to show him her right thigh.

Another intriguing story which I once heard at a ceilidh is worth recounting here because in a minor way I was involved in a sequel. It concerned an old shooting lodge which was situated in a lonely corrie some miles from Bruach and was supposed to have a haunted attic bedroom. In this lodge the river watchers stayed during the three months of the salmon fishing season but for the rest of the year it lay empty and unvisited. Though it was, it seemed, only the one bedroom that was haunted by a rather noisy ghost the watchers rejected all the rooms save the kitchen where they bunked together in front of a good bright fire. Only one man from Bruach had ever had the courage to sleep in the ghost's bedroom. This was old Finlay who told the story himself.

'They said I would never do it,' he related. 'But I knew so long as I had my bible with me I would come to no harm.' Finlay was an exceedingly devout man. 'I got into bed an' I read from the good book, an' I made sure before I settled myself down that it was right to my hand the moment I woke up. I must have gone to sleep then till about two o'clock in the mornin' an' I woke up in the dark, knowin' that the door of the room had just opened. "Is that you, Neilac?" I called out, thinkin' at first he'd come across some poachers an' needed help. There was no answer. An' then I felt a heaviness on my feet at the bottom of the bed. It came up over my

body slow an' heavy an' pressin' down. I could feel it was an
evil thing the way it was affectin' me an' I was pantin' with
the fear of it. Then I remembered my bible an' I picked it up
an' held it tight in front of me. As soon as I did that the
heaviness started to move away down again. Down an' away
from the bed an' the room, till the door closed again.'

'An' did you stay in the room?' Anna Vic asked in a hushed
voice.

'Aye, I did. An' I slept till the mornin' then.'

'I would have been out of my bed an' the room an' away
down to the kitchen in no time at all,' Hamish said with a
laugh.

Finlay nodded understandingly. 'Aye, but you have not my
faith,' he said. 'I knew so long as I held tight on to my bible
the thing, whatever it was, would be overcome. An' it was
overcome, an' that's the way of it.'

'Would you ever sleep in that room again?' asked Erchy.

'No, I would not,' replied Finlay.

Some two years after Finlay had died we heard that the
shooting lodge had been let to a party of tourists. Hector took
them and their luggage in his boat and as was expected of
him reported afterwards on their eccentricities. Early the
following morning I came across Erchy and Hector down at
the shore hauling up their boat.

'An early trip?' I commented.

'It was the doctor,' supplied Hector.

'An accident?' We were used to climbers falling in the hills.

'No, no. It was at the lodge.' Hector seemed to be sulking,
no doubt because taking a doctor was supposed to be an
errand of mercy, and he liked his errands to be more
remunerative. Erchy took up the explanation.

'It was a man from that party of tourists Hector took over
yesterday just. One of the men had a heart attack.'

'Is he very ill?'

'Aye, pretty bad, the doctor says.'

'The foolishness of some people,' I said, 'to go to an out-of-the-way place like the lodge when they're likely to be subject to heart attacks.'

'That's what I said myself to the doctor,' replied Erchy. 'He told me there was no sign of a bad heart. The man was perfectly fit.' There seemed to be some significance in the way he was looking at me and I suddenly recalled old Finlay's story.

'Aye,' said Erchy, seeing my expression. 'That was what I was after thinkin' myself, so I asked the doctor. It was quite right. The man was sleepin' in the haunted room an' it was just after two o'clock in the mornin' when they thought they heard a noise an' went to see if he was all right.'

Winter Food

THE quiet November evening was pierced by the full throated blare of the steamer's siren. I hastened to pull back the curtains and set a lamp in the window to indicate to the crew that someone was making preparations to meet them. While I drew on gumboots I searched the darkness for the port and starboard and masthead lights which should soon detach themselves from the star-studded night. The steamer was scheduled to call every six weeks bringing us bulk supplies from Glasgow but circumstances made her visits erratic. She might be delayed for days at some other port of call; the captain might be deterred by the weather conditions off the always inhospitable Bruach shore but round about the time the boat could be expected we had to be constantly vigilant. As soon as we heard the siren's warning of her approach it was necessary to indicate in some way our preparedness, otherwise the captain, seeing no sign of acknowledgment, would head straight out to sea again without pausing, leaving us to watch our much needed and long anticipated supplies being withheld for another six weeks or so. Sometimes our goods lay on the steamer for six months before we had an opportunity to collect them.

Down at the shore dinghies were already being launched amid a clatter of Gaelic and a scuffle of shingle; torches flashed over wet stones and dark seaweed; the rhythmic sound of oars in rowlocks receded as the boats drew away from the shore. There was no pier at Bruach where the steamer might come alongside and so she lay about a quarter of a mile offshore, her position marked by her lights and their spilled reflections. The waiting people ashore heard shouted instructions and exhortations from the steamer's crew coming with ringing clarity across the water. Lowering heavy goods like drums of tar, bolls of meal and weighty tea-chests over the side of the ship and down into the dinghies that clung alongside was hazardous enough in daylight. Darkness increased the risk of accident.

I leaned in the shelter of a boulder and relished the excitement which the arrival of the steamer always injected into the village, though rarely was anything but the most mundane of cargoes discharged. Townspeople might find it

difficult to believe that such things as a tea-chest full of basic
foodstuffs or a roll of wire-netting could cause any stirring of
excitement but in Bruach life was stark and pared to necessities; luxuries were neither envisaged nor demanded. It was
the arrival of necessities that gave us our thrills. We could be
as excited over the delivery of our winter stores as a town
housewife might be at the arrival of a longed-for suite of new
furniture. Similarly the appearance of a new roll of wire-
netting or a bundle of gleaming corrugated iron sheets in a
village where sheds and fences were mostly contrived of
driftwood and rusted wire was likely to cause as much interest
and admiration as the appearance of the neighbour's sleek
new car in a suburban street. Such admissions might suggest
that life in Bruach was bleak and monotonous; it was not,
but I found it unvarying to the extent that the most prosaic
event could provide me with a disproportionate amount of
pleasure. I have exalted over the delivery of a ton of shiny new
coal, and experienced a flutter of exhilaration when the
chemist substituted an unfamiliar brand of toothpaste in my
quarterly parcel.

The steamer's engine spread the bay with noise; we heard
the anchor go aboard to shouts of farewell. Her lights were
lost again amongst the stars as she steamed out to sea. There
was the sound of oars again and soon burdened boats were
scraping on the shingle. By this time Janet and Morag had
joined me and together we helped by holding the dinghies
to save them bumping about too much while the men unloaded. The tide was coming in quickly and the sea surged
and swirled round our feet in noisy white rushes that filled
our boots before we could dodge away. The breeze was light
but full of shivers and I kept one gloved hand on the gunwale
of the boat while I tucked the other under an armpit. My
shoulders were hunched with cold.

'There's two tea-chests an' a roll of wire nettin' for you,' Erchy told me.

'Aye,' I managed to acknowledge through chattering teeth.

'Are you cold?' he demanded, astonished.

I nodded.

'I'm sweatin' like I don't know what,' he confessed, and added, 'Ach, you'll be warm enough yourself by the time you've got this lot up to your house.' He lifted two tea chests out of the dinghy and dumped them on the shingle above the tide. 'I'll give you a lift with them on to your back when I've finished,' he promised and went back to continue unloading.

There was I knew in each tea-chest about a hundred-weight of groceries and despite all the experience of burden bearing I had endured since I had come to Bruach I knew that for me the feat of carrying such a load on my back was impossible.

Erchy had finished. 'All right, then,' he said. 'Have you got your rope?'

I showed him the screwdriver and hammer I had brought with me. 'I'm not proposing to carry the chests,' I said. 'I'm going to open them down here and carry it all up in easy loads.'

He was aghast. 'That's just makin' work for yourself, woman,' he chided. 'Take them up one at a time an' you'll not find it too heavy.'

'No damty fear,' I retorted.

'Ach, you English folk aren't brought up right,' he taunted and nodded to where his own mother was at that moment tying a boll of oatmeal (one hundred and forty pounds) on to her back with a thick rope. The boll was resting on a rock of convenient height and when she had adjusted the rope for her comfort she leaned forward, taking the full weight of the sack. Steadily she picked her way over the shingle and giving

us a brief greeting as she passed went on up the road. Her
home was half a mile from the shore.

'See that, now,' said Erchy. 'An' she's seventy past, so
what she can do you can do. There's more in a boll of meal
than there is in these chests.'

Erchy had once told me in the presence of his mother that
she had, in her youth, carried up two bolls of oatmeal and a
sack of flour—a total of three hundred and ninety two pounds
—in one load on her back from the shore to her house. I had
looked askance at the old lady, suspecting that Erchy was
exaggerating the story and that she, honest soul as she was,
would rush to disclaim it, but instead she smiled, flexed her
shoulders and remembered proudly: 'Aye, an' I didn't stop
for a rest till I got to the cairn.' The cairn was only about a
hundred yards from her house.

Morag went by, carrying a sack of flour on her back and
was soon followed by Janet who besides the burden of a boll
of meal also carried a five gallon drum of paraffin in each
hand. One could not say that they carried their loads effortlessly but they were not visibly distressed and had breath to
spare to call various pleasantries as they moved away into
the darkness.

'There you are,' urged Erchy. 'They don't find their loads
too heavy so you ought to manage these.' But I wouldn't
try. I could see that he thought he ought to offer to carry
them up for me but I evaded his offer by opening the chests as
soon as his back was turned. He had a fifty gallon drum of
paraffin in addition to other things to take up for himself and
I felt I could not allow him to carry my burdens as well as
his own. I loaded some of the contents of the first tea-chest
into my sack, carried it up to the cottage and went back for
another load. I was soon sweating enough to take off the
woollen scarf from round my neck. When both tea-chests

were empty I started to roll the wire-netting up the brae in the direction of my cottage, and before I had got many yards with that I had discarded my coat also and was taking advantage of every rut in the road which would hold the netting and prevent it from rolling back down the brae while I rested and panted. I had only a few more yards to push it when I heard voices behind me in the darkness. It was Janet and Morag who, having taken the first load home, had returned for another.

'Put them down,' I suggested, 'and come in and have a strupak before you take them the rest of the way.' But no, they declined, saying that the worst part of carrying was getting the loads on to their backs and off again. Once they were on their way they couldn't feel the weight so much.

'But you'll come an' have a wee ceilidh with us tomorrow night,' Janet invited.

I said I would. For the next hour I was gloatingly inspecting and stowing away tins and packages in my larder, sniffing appreciatively at the new brand of coffee and sampling biscuits from the new tin. Then I caught sight of the clock which showed that it was past midnight. Immediately I felt so tired that I wished my kitchen had been like so many of the other kitchens in Bruach where there was what was known as a 'recess bed'. There were times when it would have been wonderful just to flop on a bed and give way to sleep without even going into another room. The wish was dispelled by a preliminary thump on the door followed by a thud of boots and a hail from the porch. It was Erchy with a sack of flour on his back; had I been in my recess bed his entry would have been just as sudden and unannounced.

'Here,' he said, 'will I get to leave this in your shed till the mornin'. They're not needin' it at the house just now an' I've the paraffin to take home yet tonight.'

'Surely,' I replied and guided him round to the shed with my lamp.

'I've got the kettle on,' I told him. 'I'll make you a cup of tea if you like.'

'Aye, that would be fine,' he agreed.

'Will you take a wee dram while you're waiting?' I bent to open the door of the cupboard where I kept the whisky bottle.

'A dram? No damty fear!' Erchy sounded indignant.

'Well, you needn't sound so outraged,' I told him. 'It's not very often I hear you refuse a dram when it's offered.'

'Aye, I know that fine, but not just now. I'm off it till the New Year.'

'But New Year's nearly eight weeks yet, and you've never been able to keep off the whisky for eight days.' I stared at him quizzically. 'What's come over you?'

'I have a bet on with Johnny that I'll keep off it till the New Year, an' I'm goin' to win it.'

'What's the bet?' I asked.

'Ten pounds!'

'Johnny's pretty certain to keep his money then,' I murmured banteringly.

'He will not, then. Folks say I cannot win but I'm goin' to show them just that when I've a mind to do a thing I can do it.' His voice was stern.

'Well, good luck,' I said as he was about to depart.

'I want no good luck,' he retorted, standing in the half-open door. 'I'm miserable enough without it.'

The next day I woke up with a stiff neck, doubtless the result of discarding scarf and coat during my exertions the previous night. It was extremely painful and though I tried liniments and lotions, compresses and massage, they did little to alleviate the pain. Had I been able to sit beside the fire all day it would not have been so distressing but that was impossible. Besides hens to feed there was a recalcitrant cow to be put out and brought home each day, a task which frequently compelled me to leap suddenly forward and head her off or race backwards to retrieve her after she had successfully eluded me. On the pocked and rutted moors the chase and consequent stumbles were agonizing. I stayed indoors as much as I could and saw no-one for three days until Morag came to seek me out. I told her of my sufferings.

'I was after thinkin' there must be somethin' the matter when you didn't come to ceilidh at Janet's the other night,' she told me. 'It was a good ceilidh an' Janet was missin' you seein' you said you'd be there.'

'Tell her I was too miserable for company,' I said. 'I'll go along when this neck of mine is better.'

'You have a bad neck?' My expression must have been eloquent because she went on: 'Will I take a look at it?'

I took off my scarf and let her inspect my neck. 'I see nothin' wrong with it,' she announced.

'I didn't expect you to,' I retorted peevishly. She offered to massage it for me but her hands were like emery paper and I had soon had enough. She then suggested she should bring home my cow and I accepted gratefully. Eventually she got up to go but paused at the door and came back to resume her seat opposite me.

'I'm thinkin' you should go to old Lila with your neck,' she advised.

I was startled. 'Old Lila? Why?'

'She can cure a wryneck. That's what we call your sort of neck hereabouts,' she explained.

I was still staring at her and she turned away, looking slightly embarrassed. I recalled that her mother was supposed to have been a village healer, able to concoct medicines of

every sort and also to bestow various charms. I knew that
Morag herself had a good knowledge of these things and
wondered why she was now suggesting I should go to old
Lila who, though considered by a few people in the village to
be skilful in such matters, Morag had always affected to
despise.

'If she can cure a wryneck, why can't you, Morag?' I
asked.

'I'm not sayin' whether or no I could cure a wryneck if
I was to ask for the power. I never did that. But I know old
Lila has it.'

'How does she do it?'

'It's just the power she has,' Morag replied and there was
a hint of reproof in her tone. She rose and again went to the
door.

'And do I have to cross her palm with silver?' I asked
lightly.

She ignored the remark. 'Will I say to Lila that you'll go
to her house, then?'

Despite my scepticism I was impressed by her earnestness.
I hesitated and tried to turn and see her face; the pain made
up my mind.

'Yes, please,' I said.

'An' when will I tell her you'll come?'

'Tomorrow?' I suggested. 'The sooner the better for me.'

'Tomorrow,' repeated Morag seriously, 'if the Lord spares
you. But it had best be at the back of eleven to make sure
she's in from the cow.'

The following morning just after eleven I found myself
walking towards Lila's cottage. It was well out of the village
of Bruach and situated in the middle of the moors with only
a vague track leading to it. As I approached the squat little
house with its grey mottled walls and its black tarred iron

roof I began to wonder if I had come too early. There was a
thin fuzz of peat smoke coming from the potless chimney but
there was no sound save the hissing of the wind through the
heather and no perceptible movement until I came within a
few yards of the house and noticed the half dozen or so
poultry which were pecking desultorily around the door.
Suddenly I began to feel apprehensive. They were all
cockerels—white cockerels! My mind ranged over the appurtenances of witchcraft and I think in that moment I might
have turned for home had not my foot skidded on the slimy
ground and as I tried to avoid a stumble the pain stabbed
into my neck. Boldly I went up to the door. It opened before
I put a hand to the latch and Lila stood there with a wide and
toothless smile of welcome that instantly banished all my
misgivings. She looked reassuringly like any other old crofter
body except for her clothes which were dusty and threadbare,
giving me the impression that she had just stood there and
let the spiders weave them on to her. Her voice was a little
harsh but her eyes were kind and her manner gentle as she
told me of Morag's visit on my behalf. She asked me how my
neck was now.

'It's no better,' I admitted, trying to move it and wincing.

'Tell me, mo ghaoil.' Her eyes were on me steadily. 'Do
you think I can cure you?'

Right up to that moment I had been sceptical but now I
returned her look with equal steadiness. 'Yes,' I said
firmly.

She asked me to stand in the middle of the room and bare
my neck and when I had done this she took a pair of old-
fashioned fire-tongs which had been standing beside the
hearth. They were obviously quite cold. She stood facing me
and opening the tongs wide lowered them over my head and
held them round my neck but not touching me in any way.

'Now close your eyes,' she said. I closed my eyes and she
began to speak. It was in Gaelic and I do not know if it was
a prayer or an incantation but I noticed that the harshness
had gone from her voice. It was only a few seconds, or seemed
to me only a few seconds, before she asked, 'All right, mo
ghaoil?' I opened my eyes and twisted my neck experi-
mentally. All the pain had gone completely, and not one
trace of stiffness was left.

'That's wonderful!' I exclaimed.

Lila replaced the tongs beside the fire. 'Yes, indeed,' she
agreed. 'An' now you'll stop an' take a wee strupak.'

I called at Morag's on my way home and put on a display
of neck wiggling to show her how successful Lila's treatment
had been.

'Aye, right enough she has the power,' said Morag
reverently.

'I was a bit bothered about all those white cockerels she
had,' I said. 'In England white cockerels are supposed to
have something to do with witchcraft.'

'Witchcraft?' expostulated Morag. 'An' what would poor
Lila be doin' with witchcraft? Is it not her cousin John that's
a butcher that sends the cockerels to her to fatten up. He
buys them for nothing as chickens an' the two of them make
a deal of money out of them as grown birds when it comes to
Christmas time.'

That night, still baffled and somewhat amused by my own
participation, I nevertheless sat comfortably beside the fire
and drank a toast to Lila while I reflected on the various
faith cures I had heard of and remembered that some of the
so-called cures lasted only a few days. I hoped that Lila's
was more permanent. I am glad to say it was.

I spent Christmas in England, returning two days before
New Year's day. That evening the Bruachites came in force

so that by eleven o'clock there was a good ceilidh going. Johnny came in, brandishing a bottle of whisky.

'Where's Erchy?' he asked. But Erchy had not then arrived.

'I'm goin' to try an' make that bugger drink a dram an' lose his bet from me,' he shouted. 'I'll have to pay him ten pounds if he keeps this up.' He plunged out into the night to search for Erchy. Apparently he was unlucky in his search because a few minutes later Erchy arrived at the cottage professing not to have seen sight or sound of Johnny. He was cold sober—and that two days before New Year was for Erchy unprecedented.

'I'm goin' to win that ten pounds,' he insisted when people teased him.

'How long do you have to keep it up?' asked Hamish.

'Till six o'clock on New Year's Eve,' retorted Erchy. 'An' not before six o'clock am I goin 'to let a single dram pass my lips.'

As New Year drew closer Johnny became more desperate. 'Ten damty pounds!' he would mutter when he looked at Erchy.

At four o'clock on New Year's Eve Erchy lurched at my cottage door with a bottle of whisky more than half empty in his hand.

'Here, take your New Year now,' he exulted. 'I won't be around to give it to you later.'

'But Erchy,' I said, 'you've lost your bet. After keeping off the whisky all these weeks you've spoiled it by not waiting another couple of hours.'

Erchy was shocked. 'But if I'd done that the man would have needed to pay me ten pounds,' he pointed out.

'Well, that was the bet, wasn't it?'

'Aye, right enough, but I only did it to give the bugger a

scare. I didn't mean to keep on until the last minute so that he'd have to pay me. He's my best friend!'

'Oh, Erchy!' I said, and sat down weak with laughter.

'Johnny will be relieved,' I told him. But Bruach was Bruach. Johnny was furious.

'He only took a drink before time so that I wouldn't need to pay up,' he complained loudly. 'Does he think I can't afford to pay him ten pounds? I'll soon show him!'

Morag reported that Johnny and Erchy 'took to their fists about it' before they had settled the matter to their joint satisfaction.

Angus, the Fisherman

I was painting the window frames of my cottage when Angus, a stocky, handsome young fisherman, called to bestow on me a 'wee fry of herring'—a half dozen or more fresh and glistening fish threaded through their gills by a piece of net twine. There were more 'frys' hanging from his gory, fish scaled fingers as evidence of his benevolent intentions towards other friends.

It was early in the season for local herring and exclaiming gratefully over the gift I put down my paint tin and brush and, from what had now become force of habit, asked if he had time to take a 'wee strupak'.

'No, no,' he declined hastily. 'I'm just newly back from the sea so I'd best be gettin' to the house. The cailleach will have my potatoes in the pot waitin'.'

Angus was a member of the crew of a fishing boat which operated from the mainland port and consequently the village saw little of him during the week. Only on Friday afternoons and then only when the weather was calm enough for the boat to call at Bruach's exposed and inadequate fragment of stone jetty did Angus get home to spend the weekend with his mother, the 'cailleach'. I had no doubt she would be anxiously awaiting him with his meal ready in the pot so I did not press him to stay. Nevertheless he found time to follow me into the kitchen and to watch while I gutted and scaled the herring. I often think it is a pity that town shops pretty up their herring by removing all the scales, or perhaps there are no scales left after the fish have tossed and rubbed their way to market. Our herring coming like this straight from the fishing boat was thick with scales which shone like spangles as my knife slid under them. I put the guts into the hens' pan and was about to scrape the scales off the plate into the fire when Angus stopped me with an expletive and a restraining hand.

'You mustn't do that!' His expression was one of horror.

'Mustn't do what?' I asked.

'You must never burn herrin' scales so long as you live,' he replied.

'Bad luck?' I asked wearily.

'Aye, indeed,' confirmed Angus. 'Did nobody ever tell you?'

'I don't think I've heard of that one,' I told him. 'And by

now I've burned so many scales it can't possibly affect my luck either way.' I turned again to the fire. 'I always do burn them. I don't know quite what else to do with them.'

'This is what to do with them.' He snatched the plate from me and going outside scraped the scales on to the cobbled path in front of the door. 'The hens will get the benefit of them now,' he said.

I sighed, and checked the reproof that was on my lips. Ever since moving into my own croft I had steadfastly discouraged the poultry from approaching too close to the cottage, being determined to keep the area around the door free from their indiscriminate droppings. But it was not so much the poultry that were worrying me at this moment. I suspected that the herring scales would attract not my hens but a horde of opportunist sea gulls and their droppings were even more indiscriminate. I put the herring on a clean plate and carried them out to the shady side of the house where there was a large, flyproof cupboard. Angus followed me and watched me put the fish inside.

'That's going to be something to look forward to for my supper tonight,' I told him as I secured the door of the cupboard. I looked sideways at him. 'Nice legal fish, too.' I said with a grin.

Angus grinned in return. He was easily the most successful poacher in the village. It might have been thought that a man working all week on a fishing boat would have little inclination for fishing at weekends but it was not so with Angus. The catching of legal fish was work; the catching of illegal fish was sport. And Angus considered himself a great sportsman. Every Friday night during the salmon season he was away poaching some river and when the salmon season was over one would hear stirring tales of Angus and a few of his cronies outwitting the local gamekeeper and returning home with an illicit stag or two.

The fact that the gamekeeper was his cousin might have led some people to suspect that Angus's poaching success coupled with his ability to escape detection were not entirely due to his own astuteness. But this was far from the truth. The gamekeeper was indefatigable in his search for all such male-factors and what is more he suspected his cousin strongly. Angus knew well that if he were to be caught red-handed at the poaching the consanguinity would not ensure leniency. In fact he rather expected it might be the reverse. So while Angus took good care not to be discovered the village sat back and enjoyed the situation, and also the clandestine gifts of salmon and venison which the good hearted Angus bestowed on us from time to time.

'There'll be some grateful folk when they see what you've brought them,' I said, indicating the 'frys' still hanging from his fingers. 'Everybody's been so keen to get the croft work finished they've had no time for fishing.'

'Ach, they're not so keen on the herrin' at this time of year anyway,' he responded. 'I doubt they're a wee bitty on the oily side for them yet. They'd be keener on them if it was at the back end.'

Every year the Bruachites put down their barrel or half-barrel of salt herring for the winter but it was the autumn herring they used for this purpose. The summer herring was too rich to take salt satisfactorily—or so they maintained.

'Give me a fresh herring any day in preference to a salt one,' I told Angus. 'Even if it does result in a touch of indigestion.'

'You don't put any down yourself?' he asked, disapproving of what he considered to be my improvidence.

I did but I must confess that it was mainly the shapeliness of the small quarter barrel snug on a low shelf in my larder that gave me aesthetic rather than gastronomic pleasure.

Also it helped to establish me as less of a novice to the crofting life and I could at least answer in the affirmative when the annual enquiry came as to whether I had yet put down my herring. To the Bruachites a dish of salt herring and potatoes was in the nature of a gourmet's delight—a traditional dish that exiles recalled with great nostalgia. But like most crofting traditions it was an extremely practical one.

'You'll never go short of a meal the winter through so long as you have your own tatties an' a barrel of herrin' put by,' they assured me with great seriousness. Every winter when the poachers could offer no venison, the sea was too rough for fishing and due to either caprice or catastrophe the butcher's van did not reach the village, I would cook myself a salt herring and potatoes and with great determination try to acquire a taste for it. It invariably ended with my eating a lot of potato and leaving all but a mouthful of herring on the plate. Every spring, when the risk of being snowed up was safely over I started to feed the contents of the barrel to the poultry, boiling it up with their mash at the rate of one fish each day in case an excess of salt should have disastrous effects on their laying or even on their lives. Surprisingly too my cow liked a ration of this mash.

'It's funny it doesn't take to you,' said Angus. 'I've known folks from away that's taken to it better than salmon or trout. There's my cousin—or some relation he is—that stays with us now and again an' he tells my mother, "Give me salt herrin' every day I'm here, Auntie, for I never get the taste of it now I'm livin' among the heathen." He's a banker away in England, you see,' explained Angus with a trace of apology.

'He's welcome to his salt herring,' I said.

His grunt dissociated him from such heresy.

He waited, restlessly shifting his weight from one foot to the other. It is second nature to a fisherman to keep moving

—doubtless to combat the cold when they are on deck. We watched the over-busy bluebottles buzzing frustratedly around the cupboard, seeking any crevice where they might gain entry. I was sure there was none. Hebridean bluebottles seem to be hairier, grosser and more malignly persistent than bluebottles elsewhere. It is reputedly the preponderance of hill sheep, sometimes so casually 'dipped', combined with the abundance of bracken which gives the flies cover, that account for the heavy infestation of these pests but, whatever the reason, with no refrigerators to store food precautions to outwit them had be be meticulous. I had my outside cupboard with its door of zinc mesh. The crofters still used the old methods of burying or salting. Such things as 'skarts' and rabbits which were to be kept for only a few days were wrapped in a cloth and then put into a hole in the ground and covered with earth and sods. Fish that was not going to be eaten immediately was put in a bowl and covered with layers of coarse salt, except for skate which, because of its abrasive, ammoniacal skin, was supposed to be immune from the attentions of the flies. It could be hung out in the sun for a few hours to improve its flavour. The first time I was given skate I was advised to treat it thus but was horrified when I went to take it in to find that there were several patches of fly eggs on the skin. With rising nausea I pointed them out to Morag who had come to supervise the cooking of the fish.

'Ach, but them's nothin's,' she comforted me. 'You'll see they'll never hatch out.'

'They're not going to get the chance to hatch out,' I told her decisively. 'It's going straight back into the sea where it came from.'

'Indeed, I'll take it myself before I'll let you do that with it,' she insisted. 'You have only to scrape them off with a knife.'

I held it out at arm's length and she was happy to take it from me.

Angus began to show signs of impatience. He made trivial observations about the weather, about my hens and about my garden. Anything, it seemed, to prepare the ground for something he particularly wanted to say. I had grown accustomed now to the fact that the Bruach people always reserved the most important reason for their visit to be mentioned off-handedly as they were about to leave. I waited, studying him covertly as we exchanged more trivialities. His alliance with the sea seemed to have infected him with a permanent buoyancy both of figure and expression. His forehead was sun and windburned; the youthful ruddiness of his cheeks was not wholly submerged in a week's growth of beard; his teeth were even and white; the thick black lashes shading his eyes gave them the smoky blue of muirburn. Compressed black curls insulated the rolled edge of his knitted cap from his forehead and thigh-length boots gave flattering length to his short legs. I was thinking to myself that if Angus had had a sister she would undoubtedly have been a beauty when he spoke decisively.

'I'd best be away, then.'

I walked with him to the gate but again he hung back, calling my attention to the silver-seamed clouds that were converging on a misty sun. The sea had darkened and stilled. I had been long enough in Bruach now to consider myself a competent weather prophet.

'Thunder?' I suggested. The day had been heavy and insect-ridden as evidenced by the hundreds of tiny flies imprisoned in the fresh paint of the window sills.

'Aye, it's thunder, I doubt,' agreed Angus and began to walk up and down in the road—slowly, four paces each way. I could deduce that the clear space of his boat deck could be

measured by these paces, for no matter how extensive the
pier or the land when the fisherman waits ashore he still
moves as if he is confined by a deck. I wondered why he
still waited and cast around in my mind for some topic I
might have neglected to mention. I must not insult him by
offering payment for the fish. Had he suffered some mis-
fortune on which I should be offering condolence? But no, I
had heard of nothing. His mother was well: I had seen her
only that morning chasing a broody hen with all the vigour
of a twelve year old. None of his cows had died recently and
there had been no storms to keep his boat in harbour.

'Did you have good fishing this week?' I asked.

'Ach.' He nodded towards the sea where an offshore wind
had begun to fan ripples across the bay. 'You know what
they say about this sort of weather?'

I knew a lot of sayings about weather but I was not sure
which was applicable in the present instance.

' "East wind an' small beefies",' he explained. 'You don't
catch much when the wind's offshore. Not enough for a man
to put by,' he added meaningly.

In a flash I remembered. 'Angus! I hear you're thinking
about getting married?' I challenged him with a smile.

He half smiled in return, showing only his bottom teeth.
'You heard that?' he demanded with a quick shy look.

'Yes,' I admitted. Actually what I had heard was, 'They're
saying Angus is speakin' of marryin' this year but ach, I
believe it's all a lie for there's no sign of a bairn yet with Mairi.'

'An' who'd be after tellin' you that, now?' he enquired,
scuffing at the road with his fish scale spattered boots. His
smile was complete now, showing all his teeth and the
radiance of it filtered through his stubble like the sun through
a gorse bush.

In England in similar circumstances I should have blamed

the proverbial little bird but in Bruach the expression only aroused suspicions of my sanity.

'That's what they're after sayin',' I told him in the Bruach idiom. 'Is it true?'

'Aye well, I'm thinkin' about it right enough,' he admitted cautiously. 'Though it'll not be for a whiley yet.'

'When?' I persisted, seeing that he was anxious for me to press him.

'I'm thinkin' maybe I'll get a week before the winter herrin' comes in,' he said. 'The skipper's aimin' to take a wee holiday about then so I'd have nothin' else to do.'

'That will be about September,' I said.

'Aye, about then' he said with assumed carelessness. His manner became serious. 'Me an' Mairi, we're plannin' to do things in style when we do get married,' he confided. 'She's goin' to have a fancy white dress an' we'll be sure to see the hotel does things properly.' He paused to adjust the strings of fish, transferring them to other fingers. 'Mairi's sister is cook at the hotel so there'll be good eats, that's for sure.'

'I do hope you'll have a fine day for it,' I told him. 'It makes such a difference if the weather's good, doesn't it?'

He seemed surprised that I should consider the weather important. 'Aye,' he agreed, polite though perplexed.

'Mairi will be praying for good a day if she's going to wear white,' I explained.

His face cleared. 'I see what you mean,' he agreed. 'Aye, right enough, Mairi will be wantin' the sun to shine but for the rest of us it's no matter. What I mean is, we'll be in the car or in the church or else in the hotel an' I'm seein' that there'll be a good drink in it for everybody so I don't believe the weather's goin' to matter much at all.'

Happily he raised the strings of fish in farewell and clumped hurriedly up the brae.

The Wife of Little Ian

ALTHOUGH it was some time before Angus could think of taking time off to get married the conversation when I called at Janet's a few nights later dwelt frequently on the subject of the forthcoming wedding. The general opinion was that, at twenty-four, Angus was 'gey young to be thinkin' of marryin',' but it was accepted that his earnings, legitimate and illegitimate, were good and that he could well afford the lavish entertainment he was promising.

'There'll likely be a dance afterwards?' One of the teenage lassies spoke up, her eyes glowing with excitement.

'Indeed there will so.' Janet was emphatic. 'Angus was tellin' me he's after speakin' to the piper that's to play the "Grand March", an' to a band that's to play for the dance afterwards.'

'There'll be a good drink in it, anyway,' confirmed Erchy with a happy wink that embraced the whole company. 'He was tellin' me he's reckonin' on a bottle of whisky for each man an' a half bottle of sherry for each woman.'

'That's goin' to cost him a penny,' said Morag.

'Aye, an' that'll not be includin' the food we get besides,' added Erchy. 'He's plannin' somethin' pretty good.'

'Wis drinks like tsat, who'd be wantin' food besides?' put in Hector in his lispy Highland voice. 'He can leave tse food out of it. Tsere's no sense in wastin' money, after all.'

'It's time we had a good weddin' hereabouts,' said old Murdoch. 'It's long enough since the last one.'

'You should get married yourself if you're that keen on weddin's,' Johnny told him.

The old man's face crinkled in a sad smile. 'Ach, the sun is too far in the west for those games now, I'm thinkin',' he said regretfully, and comforted himself by vigorously knocking out his pipe.

Bean Ian Beag (the wife of little Ian) stood up. 'There's some folks finds it easy enough to make money,' she observed pettishly. 'An' they find plenty things to waste it on when they have it.' She sniffed.

'Ach, you'll no say that when you're enjoyin' yourself at the weddin',' old Murdoch soothed.

'I'll not be goin' to any weddin'.' There was a bitter edge
to her voice as she made the announcement.

'Not goin'?' exclaimed the jovial Anna Vic. 'Why ever
not? It's a shame not to go if you're invited.' She centred her
large backside more comfortably on the inadequate kitchen
chair. 'There's nothin' will keep me from goin',' she added
firmly, and then, catching Morag's eyes, added uneasily,
'Unless I break my neck first.'

'I don't see the sense of wastin' money on big swanky
weddin's,' pursued Bean Ian Beag disapprovingly, but Erchy
cut her short.

'An' there's others don't see the sense in wastin' money on
the sort of things you think is important,' he told her meaningly. Bean Ian Beag flushed. She opened the door. 'Oidhche
Mhath!' she called abruptly and pulling her cardigan close
up to her throat she took her disapproval with her into the
night.

'She's vexed,' said Morag unnecessarily.

'Let her be vexed,' said Erchy.

Bean Ian Beag's husband, Ian Beag, had died four years
previously and it had since been the often expressed desire
of his widow to provide for his grave a handsome tombstone
such as she had seen in mainland burial grounds. It was a
desire that received scant sympathy from the Bruachites, for
Ian Beag had been only a humble crofter and the few
'swanky' tombstones there were in the burial ground marked
the graves of lairds and their ladies or of wealthy tradesmen
and their families. These the crofters viewed with more
indifference than envy and if, as happened infrequently, they
felt compelled to mark the grave of a deceased relative they
would keep their eyes open as they roamed the shore or the
moors for a slab of stone of a suitable size that could be
carried home easily in a creel. Should they be really

determined they could take a pick-axe and excavate one from some rocky outcrop. There was stone enough in Bruach for all purposes, they reckoned, and you did not need to pay fancy prices for fancy shapes imported from the mainland. Once having found a slab of pleasing shape and size then you could chip out lettering if you felt it necessary and had the ability to do it. There were perhaps half a dozen such headstones in the burial ground, one or two of them quite skilfully executed, the rest crude. One verged on the comic. Old Neil had put it there in memory of his mother and whether having chipped out some of the lettering he had lacked further patience or opportunity no-one knew or would ever know for old Neil had himself passed on. But there the stone still stood proclaiming:

> 'Here lies Kate Cameron
> Wife of John McInnes
> and mother of
> 1904.'

'A tombstone's a fine thing for a widow woman to be wastin' her money on,' old Murdoch said. 'An' anyway, supposin' she does get a swanky stone who's goin' to put it up for her? It's not easy work, they tell me, an' they charge a bit for doin' it.'

All eyes turned on Erchy who, being fairly young and strong and also being related to everyone in the village, had most experience of digging in the graveyard.

'Not me,' he objected.

'Did she ask you about it?' enquired Murdoch.

'She spoke about it once,' Erchy admitted. ' "I will not then," I told her. "Them swanky tombstones is damty heavy things an' if you're so set on gettin' one from the mainland you can get men from the mainland to come an' put it up for you while you're at it!".'

'That would take her back a bit, likely?' suggested Morag.

'She was mad at me,' confirmed Erchy. ' "The dear knows, I'll never afford a stone an' pay men to come over an' set it up," she said. "Then you're wastin' your time savin' up for it," I told her. "You're not gettin' me to do it for you. Your man will lie no better or worse whether or not he has the weight of that on him",' he finished triumphantly.

'I doubt she'll no rest content till she gets one, all the same,' said old Murdoch, shaking his head.

'I don't know why she doesn't forget Ian an' take Duncan Mor from Tornish for her man,' interposed Johnny.

'Here, no,' remonstrated Morag, a flush rising on the wrinkled skin over her cheekbones.

'He's keen enough to get her, anyway,' insisted Johnny.

'Is that so?' asked Janet with a surprise that was assumed so as to elicit further information.

Everyone in Bruach knew of Duncan Mor's attendance on the widow. He was supposed to work on the roads but it was only the small stretch adjoining the widow's croft that was receiving much of his attention. He was always at hand to carry her bolls of meal from the steamer when it called; always available to scythe her hay when it was ready. He was there to 'cut' her bull calves and to strip her peats and when he had been fishing the widow was invariably given the first choice of his catch. Duncan's attempted courtship was not much commented on in Bruach but it was certainly no secret.

'He's been tryin' to talk her into marryin' him for the best part of two years now,' Johnny went on. 'You mind he was always keen on her before ever she married Ian.'

'Aye, right enough, he was,' agreed Janet.

'She didn't fancy him then an' I'm thinkin' she'll no take him now,' said Morag.

'An' why wouldn't she?' enquired Erchy. 'He's good enough for her, isn't he?'

'He's a good worker when he has a mind,' conceded Janet.

'I'm sayin' nothin' against the man himself,' argued Morag indignantly.

'Then why are you after sayin' she'll no take him?' Erchy persisted. 'Is he no "guaranteed all correct"?' There was general laughter. The phrase 'guaranteed all correct' was used at the cattle sales when a bull was put into the ring.

'He's that all right,' said Johnny. 'He gave that girl Fraser a fine son when he was workin' over on the mainland a year or two back.'

Morag looked discomfited. In explanation of her own solitary state she once confided to me that Bruach 'misliked a widow to take a second man'. I suspected now that she was voicing the aversion of her generation to second marriages rather than intending in any way to denigrate Duncan Mor's character or capabilities.

'Ach!' Morag tossed her head and the tone and the gesture were intended to dismiss the subject, but she was urged on. They were hoping no doubt that she would astonish them by disclosing some hitherto unrevealed tit-bit of scandal about Duncan.

'I told you I have nothin' against the man,' she repeated. 'But look at his face.'

'Aye, his face,' murmured Janet.

'It looks for all the world as though somebody's been walkin' over it with their tackety boots on,' Morag burst out.

'I don't see his face matters so long as he has a pound or two in his pocket,' said Erchy.

'I'm just sayin' I don't believe she'll ever take him,' replied Morag firmly.

But she was wrong.

One night several weeks later I had drunk my nightcap of hot milk, closed the book on my nightly ration of reading and turned the lamp flame low in preparation for carrying it upstairs. The hot water bottle was already between the sheets and I was indulging in my third or fourth yawn when the sneck of the door lifted and it was pushed open.

'Here,' I called.

Janet came in out of a drizzle of fine rain that shimmered on her rough tweed coat.

'Here, here,' she exclaimed, seeing my preparations for bed. 'You're surely not thinkin' of going to your bed an' missin' the party?' Janet sounded excited.

'What party?' I asked.

'Why, the new bride and bridegroom,' she elucidated.

I put down the lamp. 'What bride and bridegroom?' I demanded. 'I hadn't heard of any wedding.'

'Why, Duncan Mor's an' the widow's. Did you no hear they'd gone off to the mainland first thing this mornin' to get themselves married?'

'No, really!' I said, feeling my excitement rise.

'Aye, an' now they're back an' they've sent word round to everybody to come an' have a wee bit celebration with them. You'll surely not be missin' that?'

I turned up the lamp while I found a pair of shoes. I looked at Janet's feet and saw that she was wearing her usual gumboots. 'Is it very wet?' I asked her, doubtfully.

'Ach, it's no bad but if we're goin' to cut across the crofts you'll need boots anyway, mo ghaoil. It's what everybody will be wearin'.'

'Are they going for a honeymoon?' I asked as we set off.

'I believe they've had it,' she said. 'They went to the pictures.'

I chuckled. 'They're easily satisfied.'

'Aye, well, d'you see they'd have to be back to feed the hens anyway,' said Janet.

It was a happy enough party that had assembled at the widow's house and at four o'clock in the morning when I left they had not come to the end of the whisky and the singers were still in good voice.

As the day progressed the drizzle cleared and released a warm calm sunlight. I was full of yawns and there being no task pressingly urgent I had an early lunch, took out a waterproof and rug and stretched out luxuriously in the sun beside the stone dyke. I thought I was only allowing sensations of sleep to drift over me but I awoke to the sound of hard-breathed grunts that could have been made by old men or old horses. It was neither. Johnny and Erchy appeared round a corner of the house carrying between them a long heavy plank of wood which they had found on the shore. They dropped the plank abruptly on to the stone dyke and rubbed at their shoulders.

'My God, but there's some weight in that,' grumbled Erchy. They disdained a space on the rug and sat down on the damp grass, their backs resting against the dyke.

'Tea?' I offered, but was glad when they refused.

'Water's what I want,' said Johnny. 'Just a good drink of water.'

'I've got lemonade,' I told them. 'Made from fresh lemons.'

'Fresh?' exclaimed Erchy.

'Well, pickled fresh,' I confessed. We rarely saw a fresh lemon in Bruach but the previous day I had found half a dozen of them washed ashore. They proved only slightly salty to the taste and the lemonade I subsequently made from them was delicious. I went into the cottage and brought out bottle and glasses. They spurned the glasses and shared the bottle between them, literally pouring the liquid down their throats.

'I could have done with a drink of this last night to cool my whisky down,' said Erchy, wiping his lips.

'What time did you get home from the party?' I asked.

'Home? We didn't go home yet,' they said together and winked.

I laughed. 'You Bruachites astonish me,' I said, shaking my head. 'You seem to be able to keep going without sleep. I left the party at four o'clock and came to bed. I got about four hours sleep but I've been feeling like a limp rag all morning. That's why I brought the rug out here so that I could have a siesta.' I studied their faces and found no visible traces of their night's excesses. I knew only too well that my own face looked grey and drawn. 'I wish I knew your secret of going without sleep,' I told them with an unsuppressable yawn clipping off the last word.

'I don't go without my sleep,' retorted Erchy. 'It's just that I don't need to go to my bed to get it. I can sleep anywhere, anytime, even when I'm walkin' round.'

I looked at them doubtfully.

'That's true,' corroborated Johnny. 'I'm the same myself. Why, I can even go to sleep when I'm riding my bicycle.'

My doubts vanished. Having driven behind Johnny and his bicycle on many occasions his statement only served to confirm my suspicions.

They had finished the lemonade and I willed them to go so that I could laze for another half hour before I had to think about the afternoon's chores. Johnny produced a packet of cigarettes.

'Sho?' he offered. I refused.

'What did you do if you didn't go home after the party?'

I asked with simulated interest. 'You haven't been collecting driftwood all the time, have you?'

'No, indeed. We went to keep an eye on Duncan Mor.' They both winked heavily again.

I put the question they wanted me to ask. 'Why keep an eye on Duncan?'

'Did you no hear what was happenin' then?'

I was suddenly alert. There is nothing like the prospect of a morsel of scandal to banish sleepiness. 'I heard nothing,' I told them. 'She hasn't turned him out already, has she?'

'As good as,' Erchy replied. His eyes looked at me triumphantly through the smoke from his cigarette. He stood up. 'I think we'd best be on our way,' he said.

'Oh, come on,' I cajoled. 'Tell me what's been happening?'

He relented. 'Well, you'd be after hearin' that Bean Ian Beag said she'd only marry Duncan if he would buy a tombstone for her husband's grave?'

'No!' I replied indignantly. 'No-one mentioned a thing.'

'That's the way of it, then.'

'I wonder if he'll keep his promise now he's got her,' I murmured.

'Keep it? Indeed she'd have none of him till the stone was paid for an' delivered to the pier on the mainland. It was not till she'd inspected it that she agreed to go to the registry office with him an' have the service. They arranged when they came out of the pictures for a lorry to bring themselves home along with some whisky for the party an' the tombstone for Ian. They dropped the stone off at the burial ground on the way back.'

Erchy and Johnny tentatively lifted the plank of wood from the dyke. 'Well, I never,' I said, suppressing a giggle.

'It's a fine handsome tombstone, too,' said Erchy. 'One of

them that's got a thing like a toilet roll hangin' over the top
of it.'

'A scroll,' I murmured. 'But,' I went on, 'surely Duncan's
not going to have to erect it for her, is he?'

'Indeed he's after doin' that right now,' said Erchy. 'As
soon as the party was over last night out came Duncan Mor
with his spade an' graipe that he uses for his road mendin' an'
off he went to the burial ground.'

I started to laugh cautiously.

'We went down about an hour ago to see how he was
gettin' on an' he was near finished of it,' Johnny took up the
story. 'He had the stone up by then an' he was just stampin'
the ground down round it.' He tilted the lemonade bottle to
his lips and drained it of its last drop.

'Come to think of it, Erchy,' he added reflectively, 'he was
stampin' the ground down awful hard, wasn't he?'

Farewell to Farquhar

OUTSIDE her cottage Sheena was swishing potatoes around in a pail of water. I waited until she should notice me. The potatoes had been grown on a thick layer of manure; they had obviously been lifted in wet weather, so that much of the soil still adhered to them. When cooked they would be eaten with their skins but this meagre cleaning was all they would receive beforehand. I had to assume that it was the amount of soil she ate that kept Sheena so healthy. She looked up and saw me.

'Well, Miss Peckwitt!' she exclaimed and after wiping her hands down her rough apron she pulled me into the dim kitchen, surprising a couple of hens which darted squawking between our legs. She banished them through the open door with a lengthy admonition in Gaelic, cleared her throat once or twice and spat with masculine efficiency.

'You'll excuse me, mo ghaoil, but I have a wee bobble in my throat,' she explained as she came back inside. She shifted the kettle from the hob to a hook over the pile of peats from which there came only a faint wisp of smoke. I saw her intention.

'Sheena, I mustn't stay for a strupak,' I said hastily. 'I'm on my way up to the post office and they'll be closed if I don't hurry.'

'Ach, closed indeed!' Sheena's voice was arrogant. 'You can always go round to the back of the house an' get them to open up for you,' she said, poking vigorously at the peats with her work-toughened fingers.

'But I only want a stamp,' I told her.

'Is it a stamp? Well, isn't that what they're there to sell to you? Indeed many's the time I've had them up from their beds at night to get just that from them,' she assured me. She looked at me, perhaps expecting to see an expression of approbation. I showed none. I had already heard many complaints from the postmistress as to Sheena's late night demands.

'I only called in for a minute to say how sorry I am to hear of your brother's death,' I said.

'Aye, aye.' She allowed her voice to break with conscious emotion. 'My poor, dear brother's passed on at last.' She dabbed at her eyes with insensitive fingers, sniffed, and wiped her nose on her wrist.

It was three months since Sheena's bachelor brother Farquhar had been taken to the hospital and until then he had lived alone on the family croft inherited on the death of his parents. Alone, that is, except for a pet pigeon which at night slept in a makeshift cage beside the recess bed in the kitchen. Farquhar had been a big, handsome man of porage oats muscularity and had reputedly won prizes for various feats of strength including 'tossing the caber'. At 'sixty past' when I had first encountered him he was still a striking enough figure to be bait for romantically inclined female tourists—until they discovered he was nearly stone deaf.

Between Sheena and her brother there had, since the death of their parents, existed a state of tepid antipathy. She would call on him dutifully on the rare occasions when she was near his croft, which was at the opposite end of the village from hers, but her visits, rather than being directed towards his well-being, were more opportunities to upbraid him for not making himself available when she had need of someone to carry up her bolls of meal from the steamer, or had been desperate to gather in the hay before the threat of weeks of winter storms. Farquhar, no doubt aided by his deafness, remained loftily aloof to his sister's taunts and on his part avoided doing more than popping his head inside the doorway of her cottage to bark an abrupt 'Ciamar a tha?' by way of hail and farewell. Occasionally, if he had caught more fish than he himself could use he would, in passing, tip a few into one of the tin baths or pails that stood outside ready to catch the rain, but join his sister in a strupak or sit down even for a moment in her kitchen he would not. It was accepted in Bruach that Sheena thought her brother should feel excessively guilty because he had inherited the whole of the parental croft while she had got 'not so much as a scythe-stroke' as she put it. Her attitude towards him they believed was resentment because he displayed no evidence of any such guilt. However, when Farquhar had at last yielded to the illness that the Bruachites had for some time perceived to be affecting him and had taken to his bed, Sheena had attended him as assiduously as could be expected. It was whispered by some that her zeal was increased by a suspicion that the village nurse, who was popularly described as a frustrated spinster, might take the opportunity to make a pass at her brother while he was too weak to resist and thus perhaps gain possession of the croft. Whether or not there was any foundation for this suspicion there was no doubt that Sheena devoted herself to her brother's welfare. When, eventually, it was decided that Farquhar must go into hospital for examination, Sheena had come to call on me. Would she, she asked diffidently, 'get the loan of a couple of my cushions'?

'Of course,' I replied and hoped an explanation would be forthcoming without my having to do too much prompting.

Obligingly she had enlightened me. 'You see, Miss Peckwitt, the ambulance was to take my brother to the hospital but when he heard of it he would have none of it.' She shook her head despairingly. 'You know yourself how thrawn the man can be an' if he says he'll not do a thing then he won't. Not supposin' I stand on my head to ask him.'

'How are you going to get him there?' I asked, realising that it was going to be well nigh impossible to get an ambulance or a car across Farquhar's rough and boggy croft at this time of year.

'Well, you mind a couple of weeks back my brother an' Hamish went shares in buyin' that old lorry from the tinks that were here?'

I nodded, recalling the amused astonishment of the village when it was learned that Farquhar, the least mechanically minded man in the village, had paid good money for a ramshackle vehicle that looked as if chassis and body were trying to shake loose from each other and sounded as if the engine would be relieved if they did.

'They had this idea they was goin' to make money for themselves out of it, though I doubt all they would make would be firewood.' She gave a derisive snort. 'Now my brother's sayin' if he cannot get to hospital on his two feets he'll ride in his own lorry to get there.'

'It might be the only way to get him across the croft,' I admitted cautiously. 'But surely he's not thinking he can go all the way in it?'

'He is so,' affirmed Sheena unhappily. 'That's why we're needin' a few cushions to make him comfortable.'

I had already picked up all the cushions I possessed but Sheena stopped me. 'We're not needin' them till this evenin', mo ghaoil,' she told me. 'I'd be feared the hens would dirty them if I took them now. If you would bring them yourself over to Farquhar's house we could all see him away.'

'Certainly I will.' Evidently Farquhar's departure was going to be something of an occasion. 'What time?'

'At the back of four,' she replied and hurried away.

At four o'clock I had started out for Farquhar's croft, carrying the cushions under my arms. When I arrived the lorry was already waiting outside the cottage, an old-fashioned red plush armchair borrowed from Janet sitting in the back. Morag and Janet were among the seven or eight women who had come to watch and to help if help were needed, and three or four of Farquhar's cronies were there to give advice. And of course Johnny and Erchy. The two younger men climbed on to the lorry and adjusted the position of the chair

so that it was central with its back supported against the cab.
They stood back and surveyed it with the same care and
attention they might have given to the arranging of the
village queen's throne on a decorated carnival float. They
called to me and I handed up my cushions. Morag also
handed up two of her own. The men dumped them on the
chair.

'Not like that!' expostulated the nurse fussily, and gave
complex directions as to how the cushions should be placed.
She could not herself climb on to the lorry without aid and
had shrewdly rejected the men's offer to hoist her up.

Farquhar appeared in the doorway. He had become
pathetically weak and thin but he waved aside attempts to
help him. We all watched anxiously as, dressed in his best
suit which now hung loose on him and sporting a new cap
which intensified the sallowness of his skin, he tottered to the
lorry. There, he rested for a few moments trying to gain
strength to climb up. To the suppressed injunctions of 'wait
now!' and 'watch yourself, now, Farquhar!' he lifted first one
leg and then the other. Then his head went down on his
arms as he hung on. There were indrawn breaths of silent
sympathy as we contemplated the feeble body that until
recently had been so strong. After one or two more vain
attempts Farquhar at last allowed the men to lift him aboard,
and this they did with infinite gentleness. Solicitously they
escorted him to the chair, arranged the cushions for his
comfort and draped him with rugs. Farquhar was seen to
speak a few words to Johnny and the latter jumped down
from the lorry and went back into the cottage to emerge in a
few minutes with the pigeon in its cage. Farquhar gave the
bird a loving glance. The nurse's face turned bright red.

'Take that bird away!' she shrilled. 'He cannot take a
pigeon to hospital with him.'

Farquhar's head was sunk on his chest. He appeared not to have heard her objection.

'Take it off the lorry at once, Johnny,' she reiterated imperiously. 'Whoever heard of taking a pigeon into hospital?'

Johnny turned on her with a brusque comment which silenced her temporarily. The driver started the engine and the lorry chugged forward.

'Cheerio, Farquhar. You'll soon be back.' There was a chorus of affectionate farewells and good wishes. Surrounded by my tapestry cushions, by Morag's red paisley cushions and with his head resting on a bright orange cushion that had been one of Katy's wedding presents, the old man surveyed us. With a wan attempt at acknowledgment he raised a regal hand in salute. We trailed along behind the slow-moving lorry ready to give a hand should it get bogged. The pigeon watched us with bright eyes and a curious bobbing head. The nurse forged ahead of us towards where her own car waited to escort the lorry to the hospital.

'It's me that'll get the blame for that pigeon,' she flung at Johnny bitterly as she passed him.

'Ach, if you get blamed for nothin' worse than a pigeon you're not doin' so bad,' Johnny returned.

The nurse rushed on, caught her foot in a rabbit-hole and fell flat on her stomach.

'It's me that'll get the blame for that rabbit-hole,' Johnny mocked. She darted him a murderous glance as she picked herself up. Vexed and dishevelled she struggled on ahead. The lorry reached the road and tentatively gathered speed. The nurse's car followed decorously.

'He was a nice man, Farquhar,' said Erchy.

'Aye, I don't know that he ever harmed a man nor woman in his life,' agreed Johnny.

They spoke reverently as if they were already composing his obituary.

'We'll miss him,' contributed Old Murdoch.

'Good Heavens!' I rebuked them. 'You're all talking as if the man's going to hospital to die.' I saw their expressions. 'He's only supposed to be going for a check-up, isn't he?' I finished haltingly.

'Aye, aye, right enough,' said Old Murdoch, but I caught his tone and knew that I had been shut off from something they all knew instinctively.

The group dispersed. Morag and I walked back together.

'They seem to think it's more serious than just a check-up with Farquhar,' I taxed her.

They think it's cancer,' she said.

Aghast, I repeated the word. 'Has the doctor confirmed it?'

'Ach, indeed, I doubt the doctor wouldn't know for certain yet but I'm feared it's cancer the man has right enough. Folks was sayin' they could smell it when he first took to his bed. There's a kind of queer smell about cancer that there's no mistakin'.'

The lorry returned that evening with Farquhar's pigeon still in its cage. 'You should have seen the matron's face when Farquhar said he was for keepin' it under his bed,' Hamish the driver reported gleefully. 'Farquhar pleaded with her but she near shouted her head off about it.' Four days later, although the pigeon was given its freedom during the day and fed along with the hens just as when Farquhar was there, the poor bird was found dead.

'I believe it's died of a broken heart,' commented Morag.

Now, three months later, Farquhar was dead—of cancer, as Bruach had diagnosed. The news had come through only the previous evening and all day there had been a constant stream of sympathisers calling on Sheena. The abundance of

visitors and the consequent brewing up of strupaks was doubtless the reason why, at past five o'clock in the afternoon,
Sheena was busy cleaning potatoes for the meal she and her
son would normally have eaten around three o'clock. However, it was with impeccable courtesy that she received me and
betraying no sign that my visit was a further interruption she
insisted that I sit down if only for a 'wee minute.' She herself
sat down opposite me and after giving the kettle a glare that
should have frightened it into an immediate boil she
composed herself for grief.

'Indeed it's sad to lose one's only brother,' she said with a
heavy sigh. I murmured obsequial agreement and was on
the point of offering the platitude that her brother had lived
to the good old age of seventy-five when I remembered that
Sheena herself was the elder by five years.

'He suffered too at the end,' she said. I nodded in mute
sympathy. 'He would take no drugs, the matron told me,
but I believe he chewed terrible holes in the blankets when
the pain was bad.' She shook her head sadly.

'Did you ever hear, Miss Peckwitt, that my brother should
have died a long time ago?' she asked me with a sudden
return of animation.

'No, really?'

'Yes, as true as I'm here. The doctor that was here then
told my brother just after he was sixty-five. He'd been poorly
then for a week or two an' taken to his bed. "Farquhar,"
says the doctor to him, "I must be honest with you, man, an'
tell you that you'll not live more than six months longer".'

'What a terrible mistake!' I exclaimed.

Sheena gave an exasperated click of her tongue and
jumped up to poke at the peats. She blew on them until they
sent up a few desultory sparks before she sat down again.

'How did Farquhar take it?' I asked.

'Aye, well, Miss Peckwitt, you know how it was with Farquhar. He was that deaf he didn't hear what the doctor was tellin' him so he just went on livin' for another ten years.'

I was glad at that moment that Sheena's attention was distracted by the return of a curious hen which was pecking its way into the kitchen. She rushed at it, shooing it away with her apron.

'He has a lovely coffin,' she told me, settling herself down. 'The latest fashion, the undertaker said it was.'

I murmured conventionally.

'Aye, I've not seen the like of it before but he says it's from America an' it has a little glass window in it so that folks can see where they're goin'.'

I asked her if she would like a lift in my car to the funeral but she declined, explaining that she had hired a 'motor bust', which was her description of a taxi.

I managed to make my escape before the kettle was anywhere near the boil and continued on my way to the post office where I found the usual pre-closing cluster of dilatory customers. Erchy had just collected his mother's pension and Johnny was buying a postal order for his football pools coupon. Janet was returning to the mail order store a box containing a hat she had chosen from the catalogue and found unsuitable. On the floor behind the counter Nelly Elly, the postmistress, was pumping at a hissing primus stove on which reposed a large pan containing fish for the hens' mash. She explained that she always cooked it in the post office because if it boiled over it made such a terrible smell in the rest of the house. She rose and turned her attention to Janet's parcel which she hung on the spring balance.

'What like of hat is it?' she asked eagerly.

'Ach, it's a sort of green cloth,' Janet told her. 'They said in the catalogue it was blue but it doesn't look like the blue coat I have at all.'

'Was it for the weddin'?' asked Nelly Elly with increasing interest.

'Indeed it was,' replied Janet, 'An' I'm after tellin' them in my letter that they must send me a right blue one by return of post or I'll not buy from them again.'

'Why I was askin',' explained Nelly Elly, putting down the parcel and the spring balance, 'is that Elspeth was returnin' a hat today just to the same place. She said it was blue they'd sent her in mistake for a red one.' She lifted a parcel of a similar shape to Janet's on to the counter. 'This is it.' The two women assessed it and looked speculatively at each other.

'I wonder would it do?' asked Janet hesitantly.

'I daresay it might,' replied the postmistress.

'Elspeth wouldn't mind.' Janet sounded as if she wanted reassurance.

'Of course not,' encouraged Nelly Elly.

'Why I'm wonderin' is that I might not get another hat in time for the weddin',' Janet went on.

'It would be a pity to risk that,' said the postmistress. Janet's fingers started on the string. 'We can always tie it up again if I don't suit it,' she said.

'I'm thinkin' I wouldn't mind tryin' on your green one myself,' said Nelly Elly. 'I'd like a new hat but I couldn't make up my mind what colour I should get. Wait now till I get my catalogue.'

She disappeared into the room behind the post office and returned a moment later with a mail order catalogue folded back to a page depicting 'hats styled for glamorous matrons'. She pointed to one.

'That's the style I fancy,' she said, 'but the dear knows

what like are these colours.' She handed the catalogue to me. 'Perhaps Miss Peckwitt would know?'

Johnny and Erchy came to look over my shoulder. Erchy read out: ' "Azure", that's blue, right enough. "Hyacinth", you should know that, for aren't the wild hyacinths blue? "Walnut"—nuts is brown when they're ripe an' green when they're not so that's either brown or green. That lot's easy enough.' Erchy looked up but the two women were busily engaged in removing layers of tissue paper from the hat boxes.

'That's only three of the colours you've got sorted,' Johnny told him. 'What about this last one? "Ewer-dee-nil". What like of colour would that be, now?'

'Well, I know "ewer-dee-col-og-nee" means "smell of col-og-nee" so I would think "ewer-dee-nil" means it doesn't smell of anythin'.' He scratched his head. 'That's a damty queer name for a colour, all the same.' He turned to me. 'They don't sell hats by the smell, do they?' he demanded.

'It's the first time I've heard of it,' said Janet with a chuckle.

I explained the words and tried to describe the colour. 'You know when the mackerel have been feeding on plankton and their gall bladder turns a lovely greeny-blue?'

'Oh, aye, that's a nice colour.' They all sounded very impressed.

'That might be just the colour to go with my coat,' said Nelly Elly, 'but I doubt there's no time to send for it just now,' she added regretfully. She took Janet's hat and demanded to know if we thought she suited it. We looked at her. Nelly Elly was tall and thin with a scrubbed red face. The brim of the hat flopped coyly over one eye. Janet and I approved.

'You have the face for green,' Janet told her admiringly.

'Not like me. I'm that pale Lachlan told me I looked like a gooseberry when I put it on.'

Nelly Elly went back into the kitchen, doubtless to study the effect in a mirror.

'She doesn't look like a gooseberry in it,' Erchy said. 'She looks more like a stick of rhubarb.'

The session ended satisfactorily with Janet keeping Elspeth's blue hat and the postmistress keeping Janet's rejected green one. 'I'll explain to Elspeth on my way home,' Janet promised.

'It'll save her the postage after all,' Nelly Elly comforted.

At that moment the fish pan boiled over, enclosing us in smell of fish guts and paraffin fumes. We fled outside and Nelly Elly bolted the door after us. It was now half an hour after official closing time but it came as no surprise to us to meet other potential customers making their way in the direction of the Post Office. As always their gait was unhurried. Indeed, they seemed to consider they had plenty of time to accost us and to enquire from Erchy and Johnny, 'How did the tupping go?' and 'Did you get your stern tube sorted yet?' Janet and I walked on, exchanging reminiscences of old Farquhar.

'He was very superstitious, wasn't he?' I said.

'Superstitious!' echoed Janet. 'Indeed there was no-one like him.'

'You remember he once made a creel for me?'

'I do indeed,' replied Janet, 'an' many's the use I've seen you put that creel to since you got it.'

I smiled confirmation. 'When he brought it to the house I naturally asked him in,' I went on, 'But before he entered he stooped and put two or three large stones in the creel. 'Why the stones, Farquhar?' I asked. He shook his head at me. "Never take an empty creel into a house," he told me. "It would bring bad luck." '

'Aye, there's a deal of things like that they believe in hereabouts,' confirmed Janet. 'Like never castin' on knittin' on Fridays or you'll not finish it. That's one I stick to myself.' We walked on a little way.

'It was his English that made some of us laugh,' she recalled. 'It was as though he could never get the right hold of it at all.'

'No,' I agreed. 'Remember his "wee beefies" and his "bread loafs"?' Janet laughed.

'And I remember that year when there was a plague of earwigs. They were into everything and it was horrible.' I shuddered. 'I bought some insect spray and was spraying the bushes near the house and when I'd finished I found Farquhar had been standing there watching me. "What is that?" he asked me "Insect powder," I told him, "I'm trying to kill off a few of the earwigs." He looked at me so sorrowfully and said, "I don't believe in any of them incestitudes".'

'What's the joke?' Erchy and Johnny demanded as they caught up with us. I repeated the story.

'Aye, an' now he's bein' buried tomorrow,' said Erchy.

Johnny seemed to be struck by a sudden thought. 'How's Sheena gettin' to the funeral?' he asked. 'They're not buryin' him here so she'll need a car or somethin'.'

I told them she had already hired a taxi.

Erchy turned to Johnny. 'That's a damty good idea,' he said.

'What is?' asked Johnny.

'Let's hire a car for ourselves to go to Farquhar's funeral an' then we can go an' get drunk at the same time.'

Manure With Cream

THE impressive silver-edged invitation card to Angus's wedding eventually arrived. I opened mine under the arch scrutiny of the postman.

'Mmm. All printed,' I observed respectfully. Only once previously had I received an invitation card to a Bruach wedding but then it had been one of a batch chosen from the stationery pages of the ubiquitous mail order catalogue which supplied so many of the needs of the village. It had required much filling in by the bride's parents.

'Everybody's got one,' Postie informed me lugubriously. 'It's as bad as havin' an election when you have to take the forms round to every house.'

'It's only once in a while we have an occasion like this,' I soothed.

'Right enough, but I've creels to lift tonight yet,' he grumbled and when I offered further commiseration he added exasperatedly: 'Bloody weddin's! I don't know why they don't do the same as the tinks an' just forget about gettin' married.' Irritably he sorted through a bundle of letters. 'Why don't they go to Glasgow an' get their marryin' done without all this bother for me.'

Postie, who was by day a hard-working crofter, became the official postman only when he sighted the evening bus which brought the mails. Then he would struggle into his postman's jacket, clamp the peaked cap on his head and race to the Post Office, hoping, by taking a short cut, to reach it either at the same time as the bus or at any rate not long enough after it to give the postmistress cause for reproof. He was normally a cheery fellow but he suffered from a bad stomach which was doubtless the reason for his occasional bouts of grumpiness. Tentatively I offered him a drink of sour milk, thick and curdy, which was the accepted local palliative. He took it gratefully and refusing the glass I held drank it straight from the jug, draining it to the last gurgling mouthful. 'That'll keep me goin' for a wee whiley,' he said as he wiped the curds from his mouth with the sleeve of his jacket. 'I didn't take my potatoes yet so I was feelin' a bitty hungry.' He heaved the heavy bag of mails back on to his shoulder and departed, blowing short blasts on his whistle to inform the occupants of the next croft of his approach.

I piled damp peats on the fire so that it would stay alight for a few hours, chose one of the new loaves I had baked only that day and, wrapping it in a tea towel, set off to call on Morag who had been confined to the house for a few days after having cut her foot while haymaking. The cut had turned septic and had swelled so much she was unable to 'put a boot to her foot'. As a consequence she was having to submit to having Behag, her nephew's inefficient but sweet tempered wife, attend to her and also to the chores of the croft.

All day it had been too wet to work in the hay, the grass being repeatedly brushed with moisture from the scattered showers that drifted across the bay. Mists had screened the hills giving us glimpses of white gulls through ghosts of rain. Now the showers had been dispersed and there was a brilliant wink of sunshine that intensified the shade of the grass until it looked like green pigment while on the sea there were so many different patches of colour it looked as if the sun was shining through stained glass windows.

When I arrived at Morag's she was sitting on the bench in her kitchen with one leg resting on a pillow. The foot was swathed in damp looking bandages of a familiar but far from hygienic shade of brown. She greeted me as if it had been three years since we met instead of three days.

'And how's the foot?' I asked when I had given her the bread.

'Ach, there's hardly a thing wrong with it,' she replied. 'But Behag, the wretch has taken away my boots to stop me from gettin' about.'

'Good for Behag,' I said.

'She's not been feelin' too good in herself, Miss Peckwitt,' Bella explained. 'That's why I took them away from her.'

I looked at Morag in surprise. She was such an old stoic it was strange to hear of her suffering from anything but minor accidents.

She looked a trifle ashamed. 'Aye, right enough I wasn't feelin' in very good taste for a day or two,' she confessed, 'But I'm fine again now.' She glared at Behag. 'I would be if I could just get a hold of my boots.'

Behag tittered good humouredly.

I indicated the bandages. 'Did the doctor put that on for you?' I asked dubiously.

'Indeed, no!' she retorted swiftly. 'Why would I be wantin' the doctor an' me only havin' a poisoned foot?'

'But he was here, wasn't he?' Everyone knew the doctor had visited Morag the previous day.

'Surely he was here.'

'But the cailleach wouldn't let him look at her foot,' Behag confided.

'You should, Morag,' I scolded her. 'A poisoned foot can be very serious. You ought to have let him see it even if you won't do as he tells you.'

'An' what good would him lookin' at it do?' she asked indignantly. 'The Lord hasn't given him a face that will cure poisons.'

'You don't believe he can cure anything,' I challenged her. 'I think he's a pretty good doctor, and a lot better than Bruach deserves.'

'I believe that too,' Behag supported. 'But you can't tell the cailleach that. She thinks nothin' of him at all '

'No indeed, I wouldn't pick him up in a flittin',' announced Morag. 'He didn't come to see me as much as he came for a dram,' she added, meaningly.

'He's a right man for his dram,' murmured Behag admiringly.

'Aye,' affirmed Morag. 'Folks tell me when they go to him because they're no feelin' so well, all he says to them is, "Take a dose of water." Just that. Yet when he was here yesterday and Behag gave him his dram she asked him would he take water with it an' he pulled a sour face an' he says, "Arrah, no! Water makes me sick!"'

Behag handed me a cup of tea. There was a stong smell of manure in the kitchen and I looked down at my boots wondering if I had trodden some in when I arrived. They appeared to be quite clean. I sniffed discreetly. The smell seemed to be coming from the direction of Morag's foot.

'What are you treating your foot with?' I asked.

'I'm puttin' on it what I always use for blood poisonin',' she replied. 'It's a cure I mix for myself.'

Behag and I exchanged wry smiles. 'And what goes into it?' I pursued.

'It's a wee bitty cowdung mixed with a wee bitty fresh cream,' she explained with great dignity. 'It's what we always use for poisonin's.' I must have looked shocked for she continued reproachfully. 'You know, Miss Peckwitt, the old folks had cures for everythin' before ever there were doctors. An' there's many a one of us still believes they was the best cures. You'll see I'll be skippin' around like a young goat in a few days from now.'

Hector came in at that moment. He was carrying an ancient gun that looked as if it had been excavated from a rubbish dump but the carcases of two good-sized rabbits he carried proclaimed its efficiency. He hung them up on a convenient hook in the ceiling and pushed the gun under the bench where Morag sat.

'Well, an' how's Miss Peckwitt?' he asked, as he sat down at the table and attacked with his fingers a boiled mackerel that Behag had ladled out of the pot for him. Alternately with mouthfuls of fish he took mouthfuls of boiled potato, adeptly squeezing it from its skin into his mouth. He aimed the skins at the fire.

'Miss Beckwith's fine,' I replied. 'How's yourself?'

'Ach, I'm doin' all right.'

'An' how's Mary?' Mary, my friend from England, came each year to spend her summer holiday in Bruach.

'She's fine too,' I told him. 'At least, she was when I last heard from her.'

'Be sure an' tell her when you write tsat I was askin' after her.'

'She was asking after you,' I replied promptly.

Every time I wrote to Mary I added a P.S. with the sentence 'They told me to tell you they were asking after you'. And when Mary replied she likewise added her own P.S. 'Tell them all I was asking after them,' only now she contracted it to 'T.T.A.I.W.A.A.T.' In Bruach it was not considered sufficiently courteous to enquire as to the well being of an absent friend or relative; you must always insist that the absentee should be told you were 'askin' after them'.

Morag said, 'An' what's doin' today, Hector?'

Her nephew spoke through a mouthful of potato. 'Nossin', nossin' at all. Tse same as tsere is every osser day in Bruach.'

'There must be somethin' doin',' his aunt reprimanded him. 'Tell me if Anna Vic got her winter stack finished before the rain?'

'Aye,' replied Hector. 'Just about, tsough I reckon she'll need to take tse top off it, yet.'

'She'll be greetin' about that, then.'

'She'll no be greetin' about anytsing' for a day or two I'm tsinkin',' said Hector cryptically.

'An' why not?' Morag looked hard at him. Behag paused

in the middle of pouring out a cup of tea and looked at her husband expectantly.

'Her uncle's died in America,' Hector enlightened us. 'Tsere was a letter in tse mails tonight tellin' her so.'

'Indeed!' Morag's voice was reverent.

Behag tilted the pot and filled Hector's cup. 'I wonder did he leave Anna Vic in his will?'

Hector darted an impish glance at his aunt. 'He did', was all he said.

Morag fidgeted. 'Did you no hear what he left?' she asked struggling to sound indifferent.

'I'm tsinkin' he must have left all he had for he couldn't very well take it wiss him, could he now?' he said, disposing of the subject.

Behag reached up to the shelf above the range and took down the invitation to Angus's wedding which had been propped against the purple china clock.

'We got this tonight,' she said, displaying it in front of her husband. 'D'you think we'll need to send a reply?'

Hector's eyes opened wide. 'No, why would we?' he replied. 'Tsey know fine we'll be goin'. Why else would tsey send us an invitation?'

He pushed away his plate with its debris of bones and skin, rooted in the pocket of his jacket and brought out a crumpled packet of cigarettes. 'Sho?' he offered one to me. Behag extracted a burning peat from the fire with the tongs and lit both our cigarettes.

'Smoke, smoke, smoke,' Morag derided. 'Never happy is Hector unless he's smokin'.' Hector retaliated by pretending to aim a cigarette at her lap. She hunched away. 'Indeed I'd no spoil my lungs with it' she asseverated. 'I'm thinkin' if ever the doctors get to examine Hector they'll find him infested with nicotine.'

Hector blew smoke teasingly in her direction. Behag busied herself mixing fresh cod's livers with oatmeal before stuffing the mixture into a cod's head and baking it in the oven.

'Did you lift the paper from the bus yet?' Hector asked.

'No, I didn't yet,' replied Behag. 'Erchy said he would lift it an' give it to you later on when he'd had a read of it.'

Hector grunted.

The daily papers arrived in Bruach about seven o'clock in the evening but only three or four families took them regularly. The rest simply shared. They saw no reason to pay good money for newspapers when they would be dropping in at their friends' houses where the paper would be at their disposal. One result of this small economy was that you never saw a discarded newspaper in Bruach. All papers were eagerly sought after and cherished and when we received goods by post much of the fun of unpacking them was because they were often stuffed with newspapers which we could smooth out and read no matter how ancient the news might be. Once read the papers would be folded carefully and saved for reference, as reading matter for our friends and ultimately for re-use as packing if we should need to send anything away ourselves.

There was a noise of footsteps outside and Erchy came in followed by his dog. The dog assessed the company and seeming to find it unattractive took himself off to lie outside. Hebridean sheepdogs are primarily workers and though they are often welcome to share the home of their owners they seem to be unable to shed, even temporarily, their role of sheep watching and prefer to be outside where, when there are no sheep, they can watch or practise their tactics on cattle or hens.

Erchy threw a newspaper on the table in front of Hector.

'Did you get a read of it?' asked Hector thoughtfully.

'Aye, I'm finished with it.' Erchy sat down beside Morag on the bench and lit a cigarette 'I see you have your invitation,' he remarked

'We did,' said Behag, picking it up and admiring it. 'It's a right grand one too.' She looked at Erchy. 'Are you goin' to answer it?' she asked him.

'Answer it?'

'Well, it does say R.S.V.P. on it an' folks say that means you're supposed to answer it,' she explained.

'Ach, them sort of things is not for Bruach,' he assured her. 'It doesn't mean us. There'd be no reason why we wouldn't go, after all.'

There was a short silence while Hector studied the paper and then he pushed it aside.

'Were you out with the gun today?' Erchy asked him.

'Aye.' Hector indicated the rabbits. 'I got tse two just.'

'In the glen?'

'No. Over in tse corrie.'

'What took you there?' Erchy was curious.

'I had to take tse pollis over to Rhuna. Did you not hear about it?'

'How would I hear of it an' me away on the hill after the sheep all day?' replied Erchy resentfully.

'Aye, well, tse pollis came for me to take tsem over for sometsin' or osser.' Hector chuckled. 'One of tsem had a right queer gun wiss him too, I can tell you.'

'A gun?'

'Aye, if you can call it a gun. I knew nossin' of it till he said, "Hector", says he, "will tsere be a chance of a shot at a skart or sometsin' for dinner on tse way?"

' "Tsere might be," I told him. "If you have a gun". I

didn't want tsem to see tse one I have under tse seat,' he
added with an engaging smile.

' "I have a gun", says tse copper an' he pulls out tsis tsing
from under his coat. I near laughed out loud when I saw it.
It was from some war, or sometsin', he said.

' "What sort of ammo would a gun like tsat take?" I
asked him. "I've never seen tse like of it before.'

' "Tsese is tse ammo", he says an' puts his hand in his
trouser pocket to get it out. Tsen I see his face go all queer.
"Amn't I tse fool?" says he. "I've lost tse bloody ammo".
He felt in all his pockets wissout findin' it. Tsen tse osser
copper says to him, "I know what's happened to your ammo".

' "What?" he asks.

' "You mind tsis mornin' we had to go an' look for yon
woman tsat had gone boatin' an' not turned up again? We
tsought she'd been drowned an' tse boat might have been
washed ashore in tsem rocks an' we had to wade out to tsem?"

' "Aye," says tse osser pollis.

' "Well, you mind you went home an' changed your
trousers afterwards", tse one reminded him. "Tsat's where
your ammo will be".

' "Oh God!" he says. "Tsat will be tse way of it." '

'An' what happened to the woman?' asked Morag. 'Did
they find her?'

'Aye, tsey found her later on. She'd lost her oars an' tse
boat was blown well out to sea.'

'An' was she out all night?' cried Behag.

'Aye.'

'I hope she had plenty of clothes on,' I said. 'It was cold
last night for the time of year.'

'She had nossin' on but a basing costume, so tsey told me,'
said Hector. 'An' no much of a one at tsat.'

'And was she all right when they found her?' I asked.

Hector thought for a moment. 'I tsink tsey said she was a wee bit exposed,' he replied.

'Oh well, I'm glad they found her, the poor soul,' said Behag with relief. 'She might have been drowned.'

'You should have heard tsem pollis cursin' her for it tsough,' Hector told her. 'Wiss tsem not gettin' a skart an' after bringin' tse gun specially.' He lifted up a foot and obediently Behag knelt and pulled off his boot.

'I'm wonderin' why the pollis had to go to Rhuna,' Morag probed.

Hector wiped his hand over his chin and there was a gleam of mischief in his eyes.

'Tsey've lost tse bull,' he told his aunt. 'So tsey sent for tse pollis to see what tsey could do.'

'Is that true?' she asked.

'Aye,' he affirmed. 'My, but I got a laugh when we was comin' back an' one of tse pollis says to tse osser, "It's a shame right enough you have no ammo for tsat gun. Just look at tsat raft of skarts over tsere." He was right too, tsere was seventy of tsem if tsere was one. I was wishin' tsem pollis anywhere but in my boat so I could have a shot at tsem myself.' He poured himself out another cup of tea.

'Tsen one of tsem says to me, "Hector", he says, "are you sure you have no gun aboard yourself?" Ach well, tse man was sittin' on it if he had but known but I couldn't tell him tsat. Tsen I got a scare when I tsought maybe tsey'd heard me shootin' at the rabbits while I was waitin' for tsem in Rhuna. I was just tsinkin' tsey was goin' to start askin' more questions when suddenly one of tsem jumps up. "My God!" says he. "Tsat ammo! I just remembered it was in my trouser pockets an' I gave tsem to my wife to dry for me. She usually puts tsem in tse oven or in front of tse fire". The other pollis just laughs. "Never mind", he tells him, "you

can always claim for a new pair if tsey're too badly
damaged!" '

Johnny arrived, whistling his way in from the shadowed
sunlight. 'Aye, aye,' he greeted us and picking up Hector's
paper sat himself down in a corner to read it.

'I see that school teacher that was here once stayin' with
Janet has got married,' he said, looking up. They identified the
man for me and dismissed him as being a Roman Catholic.

'My God!' said Johnny. 'It would be a queer weddin' if
it was a Roman Catholic one.'

I looked up in surprise. I found the Bruachites' vehement
prejudice against Roman Catholics a startling contrast to
their usual tolerance.

'Didn't me an' Angus go to a Papist weddin' once,' Johnny
went on. 'One of his crew married a Roman Catholic girl an'
we went away down to the weddin'. I never saw the like of it.
The church didn't look like a church an' the fellow that was
takin' the service, the priest they called him, he was laughin'
an' jokin' just the same as if he wasn't religious at all.'

'Oh my, my,' murmured Morag and Behag.

'Aye, it's true,' said Johnny. 'He met us on the steps an'
asks us if we're guests at the weddin'. When we told him we
was he said to follow him. We did that an' he took us into
this place that looked more like a garage. It was cold as I
don't know what an' he saw we was shiverin' so he brought
one of them electric fires for us an' put it on one of the
seats. Honest, we could smell the varnish burnin' with it.
Then he went up to the front of the church an' he said,
"Would you like a record on while we're waitin' for the
bride?" He had a gramophone there an' he put on "Mairi's
weddin'." He was playin' about doin' somethin' an' suddenly
he claps his hands an' he says, "Oh God! I forgot the holy
water", an' he's away out of the church with his robes flyin'

behind him. While he's away the bride turns up an' findin'
nobody there to meet her she walks up the aisle an' just
stands there waitin'. The door of the church bangs open an'
the priest shouts, "Stand up, everybody, for the entry of the
bride!" We all stand up but he saw she was there so he says,
"All right, I see she's here so you can all sit down again".'

'What a weddin'!' disapproved Morag.

'Aye, indeed,' Johnny agreed.

'Was the bride in white?' asked Behag.

'White or some colour,' said Johnny. 'An' that was another
thing. I told you this priest put the electric fire on one of the
seats?'

We nodded.

'Aye, well suddenly he notices the bride is shiverin'. "Are
you cold?" he asks her right in the middle of the ceremony.
She nods. "Then I'll get you the fire", he says an' looks
around. "What did I do with that fire?" he asks. Well by
this time the seat was nearly beginnin' to burn, he only has
to sniff to find it. "Ah, I remember now", he says, an' takes
away the fire. He puts it so close to the bride she's havin' to
move away from it while he's readin' the service for fear it
sets fire to her dress.'

'That was no right weddin',' said Erchy.

'It was a good time we had after it all the same,' Johnny
told him. 'By God! but the whisky flowed that night an' the
wee priest had his share too.'

Morag shook her head. 'A priest,' she said, her voice full
of condemnation.

'Aye,' said Johnny, 'but d'you know the people thought the
world of him, true as I'm here. You'd never get a minister
from our church to have people sayin' as nice things about
him as they were sayin' about their priest. Not an' meanin'
them too,' he added.

Poacher's Wedding

IT WAS less than a week to Angus's wedding and as the days passed the Bruachites hastened to finish their haymaking or at least get it in weatherproof cocks so that they would not feel guilty at taking time off for the great day. Morag, Behag and Erchy had been helping me finish my winter stack and afterwards we sat in the cottage drinking tea. Hector,

doubtless having prospected and seen that the work was over,
ambled in and joined us. I showed them the wedding present
I had bought. They admired it dutifully but even after years
of familiarity with them I could not tell if they really
approved.

'I'm thinkin' Sarah will be at the weddin',' said Erchy.

'Sarah? What makes you think that?'

Sarah rarely went outside the boundaries of the village.

'I saw her comin' away from the Post office an' she had a
proper list to starboard,' Erchy told us. He was referring to the
fact that Sarah collected her pension only when the post
mistress complained she couldn't sleep at night because there
was too much money lying in the Post office (sometimes as
much as five pounds). Then Sarah would leave her croft for
half an hour to collect her dues. As she never recognized
notes as money Sarah always insisted on being paid in silver
and as her purse was a pocket inside the leg of her buttoned
knickers her financial position could always be detected by
the way she walked.

Behag tittered. 'You'd think she'd use a purse like other
folks,' she said.

'Sarah will never trust anythin' but the leg of her knickers
to keep it safe,' Morag told her.

'Aye well, at her age I daresay it's safe enough,' said Erchy.

'Too safe,' I said. I had once chaperoned Sarah on a trip
to the mainland dentist. It had been necessary to take a bus
from the port and when we came to pay the fare to the
strange driver he found he could not change my pound note.
I managed to find enough silver to pay for myself but when
he asked Sarah for her fare she handed him a shilling.

'The fare is two shillings,' he told her.

Sarah was indignant. 'It was only one shilling when I was
last on this bus,' she argued.

'It's been two shillings ever since I've been drivin' it,' the driver told her, 'an' that's twelve years now.'

Sarah flushed. 'I'll give it to you when you stop the bus,' she promised.

Now the trouble was that Sarah, when she did venture anywhere, used to work out exactly how much money she expected to need for her trip. Bus fare, ferry fare, so much for purchases, would be wrapped up separately in a twist of paper and kept in a tin at the bottom of her shopping bag. Money set side for emergencies was tucked securely up her knicker leg. Confronted now with the demand from the driver she was both embarrassed and indignant. When the bus stopped Sarah and I got out and went round to the back. the driver, obviously suspecting we might be using this as a ruse for not paying, came to keep an eye on us. Sarah started to root up her layers of long skirts and unbutton the leg of her breeches, all the while glowering at the driver until he turned his back. Eventually she managed to extract another shilling. She handed it to him and he studied it closely. There was a slight relaxing of his expression as he said, '1920. By God, you've had it up there long enough.'

That was not the only time I had been involved in an episode with Sarah's knickers. I met her one day when she was taking her cow to the bull. She seemed very distressed, frequently stopping to sit down on the side of the road and trying to straighten her bent back.

'Are you all right, Sarah?' I asked her.

'Indeed I was all right this mornin' but there's somethin' wrong with me now,' she complained.

'I'll take the cow on for you if you'd like to go back home,' I offered.

'Well, if you'd just keep an eye on her while I go an' pee

I'll be grateful,' she replied. 'It's maybe just that is the matter with me.'

I walked behind an all too eager cow and in a few minutes Sarah was catching up with me with a greatly relieved expression. I looked at her questioningly.

'Ach, here's me thinkin' maybe it was my stomach that was wrong, or maybe my heart, or my back, but when I went to pee I found it was only that I had my knickers on back to front. I changed them round an' I'm feelin' fine now.'

Erchy said, 'I reckon Angus an' Mairi will do pretty well out of their weddin'. Folks seem to be set on givin' them good presents to help with the do he's plannin'.' Mostly the Bruachites gave envelopes of money to the groom actually at the wedding.

'Not Tearlaich won't,' interposed Hector with his meaning smile.

'Why not Tearlaich?' asked Morag.

'Ach, he's greetin about tse laird cheatin' him.'

'Right enough he's lost out this time by it,' Erchy affirmed with a chuckle.

'Was he claimin' for his corn again, then?' Morag asked.

'Aye.'

Tearlaich owned one of the outlying crofts which adjoined the grazing. When the corn he had sown had grown to a tempting height it had been known for the deer to come down from the hills, leap the fence and plunder his crop. As the laird owned the deer he was responsible for any damage they did and being a generous laird he had always paid Tearlaich's assessment of the damage without quibble. Tearlaich soon made it a habit to claim every year and every year the compensation was forthcoming.

'He claimed again,' Erchy said, 'but he got word the laird was comin' to inspect it this time. It's never happened before

an' Tearlaich knew the man was suspicious. He had to run
an' get his cows an' drive them through his corn before the
laird turned up.'

'And did he get away with it?'

'He did not, then. One of the cows left a pat behind it an'
the laird saw it. He may be daft but he can tell the difference
between cow dung an' deer muck, so he turned on Tearlaich
an' threatened him.'

'The man deserves it!' said Morag.

'The trouble is Tearlaich's fairly ravin' because when the
deer get in another year he won't dare to complain ever
again,' said Erchy.

No-one had much sympathy for the perfidious Tearlaich
who spent nine tenths of his time belittling the gentry and
nine tenths of his income aping them.

'So tsat's one that will not have so much to spare for tse
weddin' present,' said Hector. 'An' here's anosser.' He
indicated himself.

'Oh be quiet!' his wife told him. In Bruach the expression
'Oh be quiet' was used in the same way as English people say
'you don't say!'. Disconcerting as it may sound to a stranger
it nevertheless invites further revelations.

'Aye, I'm feelin' tsat poor I wish I could rob a bank,'
Hector told her. Morag murmured condemnation.

'Would you throw me out if I did?' he taxed her.

'Indeed I would.'

Hector turned to his wife. 'Behag wouldn't, would you
Behag?' he asked. 'You'd never give me away.'

Behag smiled at him fondly. 'It depends,' she told him.

'Depends on what?'

'How you did it,' she replied gently. 'So long as you didn't
hurt anybody I'd hide you an' lie for you, but once I heard you
had laid a hand on a body then you would be on your own.'

'Well nobody's robbin' any banks,' said Morag, standing up. 'An' there's hens needin' to be fed an' cows to be milked.' As she had predicted she was now 'skippin' around like a young goat.'

The morning of Angus's wedding dawned with autumnal scarves of mist that were threaded with rainbows. Bruach was astir early and busy about its chores. The moors rang with the scolding voices of humans and dogs as stubborn cows were coaxed and coerced into haste. It was a good day for the wedding, Bruach allowed, because the weather was such that they felt no compulsion to resist the lure of the festivity in order to ensure the safety of the hay harvest. I had by this time retrieved my long absent car, 'Joanna', from the clutches of the mainland garage where it had been undergoing a thorough, and thoroughly prolonged, over-haul and as I had promised to take Morag, Behag and Hector to the church I set off in good time, announcing my arrival at their cottage by a few toots on the horn. Morag emerged but then found it necessary to go inside again; she and Behag came out together and Behag had to go back. When at last they were both settled in the car we sat waiting for Hector who finally 'sprackled' from the house, looking very self-conscious in his best clothes.

'Here's you keepin' Miss Peckwitt waitin' again,' Morag chided him.

'Ach, it was no my fault. Did you tell her tse reason for it?'

'I did not, then.' Behag spoke quietly.

'Aye, well you see, Miss Peckwitt, it was like tsis. Behag put out my shirt on tse line to take out tse creases an' didn't a bloody gull go an' shit on it.' Hector was outraged.

'Ach, an' you makin' such a fuss of it,' returned Morag contemptuously. 'It was only on the tail of it that it shit an' nobody was goin' to see it there.'

Most of the Bruachites had gone by specially hired bus and when we arrived the church was nearly full. The stately red-haired Mairi was stunning in her white dress and clouds of veiling and Angus, though he looked extremely tired, was a proud and determined groom. The minister hurried the service a little, I thought, and when it was over and it was time for the couple to leave the church he did not suggest that they wait until the vicious squall which greeted them had passed away.

'Ach, he's in a hurry for his dram,' Johnny excused him when I commented on this.

At the hotel we sat down to a lunch of fresh salmon and vegetables. The helpings were lavish.

'Fresh salmon,' I murmured appreciatively. 'He's not sparing any expense at this wedding, is he?'

'Expense?' Morag looked at me pityingly. 'Indeed, where would there be expense when he hasn't seen his bed for the last three nights with all the poachin' he's been doin.''

'So that's why he looked so tired,' I exclaimed.

'That's the way of it,' she said.

I looked along the seated lines of guests who were tucking in with excellent appetites. There was only one figure who appeared not to be enjoying the repast quite so much as the others. Not surprisingly, perhaps, it was the gamekeeper.

The waitresses filled our glasses with whisky and during the rest of the meal and throughout the toasts and speeches they were being continually refilled. The telegrams were read out.

'Very disappointin',' Morag commented when they had come to an end and she had detected no lewdness.

'Mairi told the best man not to read the good ones,' Erchy explained. 'We can read them ourselves when the minister's out of the way.'

Soon the singing began, appropriately enough with

'Mairi's Wedding' and from then on it was just a splendid ceilidh with anyone standing up and 'giving us a song' and everyone joining in the chorus. Jokes were screamed across the room and followed by guffaws of laughter. The tables were cleared and we danced, the bride and bridegroom leading on to the floor. Mairi was very regal, but as the rest of the gathering became more boisterous someone managed to tread on her veil. She was on her way upstairs to take it off when a voice arrested her.

'Now, Mairi my girl, watch out what you do with all that net. We'll be needin' it for the herrin' on Monday.'

When she came downstairs again Mairi was dressed for travelling. Angus joined her and the guests thronged around the couple with handshakes, kisses and farewells. 'A grand weddin',' they told Angus. 'I don't know when I enjoyed myself so much.' Only the gamekeeper stood on the edge of the crowd, aloof from all the compliments. At last it was time for the couple to go. Angus caught the gamekeeper's eye.

'Well, are you enjoyin' yourself?' he asked him.

'I am fine,' replied the gamekeeper levelly.

'Good,' said Angus. 'An' you enjoyed your dinner?'

'I did,' said the gamekeeper. 'I fairly enjoyed it.'

'That's good,' Angus told him pertly. 'For there's that bloody much of it left over it looks as if the village is goin' to be feastin' on it for a week yet.' He winked and turned again to his bride, pulling her out through the storm of confetti to the car.

'Well, well,' Morag greeted me next day. 'It's back to porridge an' old clothes for us after all the festivities.'

'It was a good wedding,' I said.

'Aye, indeed. They said at the bar they sold more half bottles of whisky than half pints of beer. That's always a sign folks is enjoyin' themselves.'

'I'd like to have a rough estimate of just how much was drunk,' I said. 'Certainly the hotel keepers must have been pretty pleased with themselves.'

'I'm thinkin' they can be pretty pleased with Angus for all the trade he gave them,' she said.

From the shore came the sound of a klaxon horn. We turned and saw it was the fishing boat on which Angus normally worked.

'I wonder why she's coming in today?' I murmured.

'To pick up Angus,' explained Morag.

'Angus? But he's away on his honeymoon.'

'He is not.' She nodded towards a familiar figure hurrying down to the shore with a bundle under his arm. Angus gave us a cheery wave.

'But I saw him go off on his honeymoon with his bride last night, 'I insisted. 'Mairi herself told me it was to be for a week.'

'You saw him go but it was only to see Mairi off from the mainland station,' Morag told me. 'Angus couldn't spare the time to go for a honeymoon just now, after havin' time off for the poachin' an' all, so Mairi's just had to go by herself.'

A Day in the Hills

I was feeling very sorry for myself. For two days I had been in bed, sleeping, vomiting and sweating my way through a bout of influenza. By the afternoon of the third day, however, I felt rather better. The nurse, whose attentions had been confined mostly to brewing herself cups of tea which she drank sitting beside my bed while comforting me with

stories of the high incidence of tuberculosis in the village and
congratulating me on my good fortune in enjoying her
devoted ministrations, withdrew the thermometer from my
mouth and announced that I might sit up. She propped me
up with pillows before she left and I listened for the sound of
her retreating car before reaching for a dressing gown. The
bedroom was beset by irrepressible draughts and chilly
despite the hissing of the paraffin stove which though
efficient enough when well pumped wilted and popped
despairingly every couple of hours demanding renewed
pumping or that its jet be pricked. Outside the wind hissed
through the leafless rowan tree and rain and hailstones
rapped aggressively at the roof and window. I thought of
the cosiness of the kitchen and resolved to make my way
downstairs.

I was standing beside the bed, gathering strength, when I
heard a shout from the bottom of the stairs.

'Bella's wantin' to know do you need anytsin'?' Bella and
Morag had been attending to the chores while I had been in
bed.

'Bless you, Hector,' I called back. 'I'm getting up. If you
wouldn't mind seeing that my coal and peat pails are full I'd
be very grateful.'

'Right, I'll tell her,' came the reply and a moment later I
heard the door bang.

'Oh, Hector,' I mused, 'you lazy rascal. Couldn't you have
seen to that little job yourself?' The door banged again and
to my surprise there came two distinct thuds of full pails on
the floor. For once I had misjudged Hector it seemed.

I continued downstairs, appreciating the comfort there is
in the sound of pails of fuel being thumped on the floor on a
winter evening. The lighting of the lamp, the clatter of
dishes, the stoking of the fire, all make the pattern of the

evening, but it is this thump of deposited pails that separates like an emphatic punctuation mark the end of the day's work and the beginning of the hours of relaxation.

I was ready with words of thanks on my lips to greet Hector, but it was not Hector who was standing beside the pails. It was Erchy.

'I could have sworn it was Hector calling upstairs to me,' I said. 'Really, I think my head must still be a bit muzzy.'

'So it was Hector,' Erchy told me. 'I was here too an' heard what you said.' He pushed the pails well to the side of the fire. 'I doubt Hector would get the peats for you supposin' you'd been freezin' to death.'

I grinned. 'I must say I was surprised when I thought he'd done it. But Hector does surprise me sometimes.' I was about to go on when the door opened and Hector himself stood there, smiling ingenuously.

'I tsought I might just as well fill your pails myself, save Bella doin' it,' he began. His glance lit, as if by accident, on the full pails and his eyes widened in well affected surprise. 'Tsey're full!' he exclaimed and came forward to warm himself at the well-stoked fire. Erchy and I looked at each other.

'Aye, the fairies filled them,' said Erchy drily.

Hector took three mugs down from the dresser. 'I daresay you're feelin' like a cup of tea,' he said, and lifted the kettle on to the fire. Seemingly exhausted by this effort he flopped into a chair.

'There's a lot of it about,' Erchy remarked.

'A lot of what?'

'This cold an' sickness they're after callin' 'flu,' he replied. 'Indeed I had it myself for a while. It was just as if I was like to faint every time I got up from a chair or out of my bed.'

'What did you take for it?' I asked.

'Ach, a good dose of whisky. There's nothin' better.'

'We should go back to makin' our own whisky, if we had
any sense,' Hector said. 'Tsere was never any colds nor 'flu
tsat I heard of when everybody kept a firkin of whisky beside
tse fire an' just took a wee dram when tsey came away from
the storms.'

'I don't know why tsey stopped us makin' it,' grumbled
Erchy. 'Nobody took any harm from it.'

'Tsey had to stop us because tsey had to stop tse English
from doin' it,' explained Hector.

I looked at him enquiringly.

'Aye well, some of tsese Englishmen, if tsey get at much
whisky tsey go prancin' after tse women like billygoats. Tsey
go mad, just.'

This explanation coming from Hector of all people almost
caused me to laugh out loud.

'It's different here,' he went on. 'In tsese parts takin' a
good dram is for when a man wants a medicine or when he
wants to enjoy himself. Not for when he's obligin' tse
women.'

There were times when remarks made by the Bruachites
left me temporarily breathless. This was one of them, though
I knew it was generally accepted among them that women
were more strongly sexed than men and suffered more if
their desire was unfulfilled.

Hurriedly Erchy reverted to the subject of colds. 'I mind
my grandfather boastin' he never took a cold in his life,' he
said.

'Aye, but your grandfather knew where was tse whisky,'
Hector told him and turning round in his chair he gave me
an expressive wink.

I responded with a smile. Well within the memories of
some of the older Bruachites whisky had been buried beneath
the earth floors of the houses and byres to keep it safe from

thieves and customs men. As a result, when the young folk had inherited the old houses and modernised them by putting in wood floors they had occasionally unearthed a secret store. Erchy's grandfather was known to have been even more cautious. Having found a large cask of whisky washed ashore he had taken it by boat and hidden it in a secret cave known only to himself. Soon afterwards the old man had died quite suddenly and though with his last breath he had managed to gasp out his secret his instructions for finding the cave were so confused that his sons, despite exhaustive searching, had never succeeded in locating it. Now the cave and its treasure had become a perpetual lure for his grandson, Erchy, and his cronies and whenever they found themselves in the supposed vicinity of the hiding place they dedicated themselves to searching for the cave, re-assessing its probable situation and making plans for what they would do with the whisky when they eventually found it. They dreamed of success in their search as other people dream of winning the football pools. They sought the cave as other men have sought El Dorado.

'If my grandfather's ghost came back that's the only question I'd have for him,' said Erchy. ' "Where did you hide that cask of whisky?" I'd say.'

'What good would the whisky be after all these years?' I asked. 'Surely the cask would have disintegrated by now, anyway?'

'I'll not rest content until I know for sure,' retorted Erchy. 'After all, to lose a cask of whisky is almost like losin' a relative.'

'Only worse,' said Hector gloomily.

'Was it the whisky you were looking for the last time I came to the hills with you? You remember, the time I saw the nun?'

'Of course,' said Erchy. 'You were as white as a sheet when you got back to the boat. I mind that fine.'

'I'd had a very disturbing experience,' I admitted.

It had been a day of late September. A calm day of gentle sunshine that lit the moors with scotch-broth colours, and I should have liked to have sat with my paint-box and brushes and tried to capture the quality of it all. Instead I prepared myself for a four mile walk to a glen where I hoped I should be able to gather blackberries. Erchy and Hector, shepherding a party of climbers down to the boat, passed the cottage and seeing me called out asking if I wished to join them. Where they were going, they assured me, there were bushes heavy with ripe brambles, all easily accessible. They would help me pick, they said, if I would make them some jam. The prospect was irresistible. I grabbed some food, a pail and a basket and followed them down to the shore.

The brambles were indeed large and prolific. With Erchy and I picking seriously and Hector remembering occasionally to pop a berry into the pail instead of into his mouth we soon had both pail and basket brimming full.

'We'll take these back to the boat if you want a look round,' Erchy offered. 'So long as you're back within the hour we'll still be here.'

'Where are you going?' I asked.

'Ach, we're away to look for somethin',' he said off-handedly.

'All right, I'll be back,' I told them and taking my packet of food I scrambled over the rocks towards the sheep path that would take me by a not too demanding way up to the nearest corrie. There in the sheltered warmth I ate my lunch and dozed for a while. When I awoke I perceived high on a distant ridge the party of climbers we had brought with us in the boat. I lifted my binoculars and watched the attenuated line of tiny figures moving slowly towards a vast, bare-looking face of rock that stood sheer above the tumbled jagged floor of the glen. I focussed my glasses on the rock face, attempting to assess its hazards, and caught my breath. I found I was staring at a shape like a great crucifix that appeared to stand out from the rock. It was an enormous, primitive carving of a cross, the Christ heavy-limbed and crooked. It was strangely lit so that it seemed to shimmer against its background. I lowered the binoculars, rubbed my eyes and looked again but now it was only the face of the rock I could see with outlines of cracks and fissures which, I told myself, might in certain lights have caused the phenomenon. Trying to shake off the feeling that I had seen a vision, I leaped up and hurried back towards the boat, but before I had gone more than a hundred yards I was jolted back into uneasiness by coming face to face with the hurrying figure of a nun. To meet a black-habited nun roaming in such a wild and desolate place is startling enough; to meet a hurrying nun with black habit flying about her shook me so much I involuntarily drew back as she passed. Then I fled.

The sight of Erchy and Hector standing nonchalantly beside the boat awaiting my arrival was immensely reassuring. Hector came forward and gallantly helped me over the seaweed-covered rocks, and I found myself glad to hold tight to the muscular arm I could feel beneath his jacket sleeve. Erchy went up to untie the rope in preparation for casting off. I could feel his curiosity. He came back to the boat without untying her.

'Ach I'm thinkin' we'll make a cup of tea before we go. There's plenty time,' he said, and shot me a puzzled look. 'You look cold,' he went on, 'though God knows why you'd be cold on a day like this.'

Not until he spoke did I realise I was in fact trembling. I

wondered whether to tell them what I had seen and if I did whether they would suspect I was suffering from hallucinations.

Back in Bruach it was a great relief to see my nun sitting in the sunshine outside Janet's house drinking tea and eating scones. There was nothing hallucinatory about her appetite.

'I met that nun up in the hills just a wee while back,' I confided to Erchy. He nodded affirmatively.

'Aye, no doubt you would. She hired Johnny's boat to take her all by herself. She said she just wanted the half hour there an' then he was to bring her back again. They were back just about an hour before ourselves.'

So was the mystery of the nun's appearance resolved but the strange phenomenon of the crucifix, though I had explained it satisfactorily to myself, still left me vaguely disturbed. In my mind I associated the vision with the party of climbers and could not rid myself of a recurring fear that I had been given warning of some fatal accident. Unable to sleep that night for wondering if they had all reached their destination safely, I listened avidly to the news the following morning in case there should be word of climbing fatalities. I questioned anyone who was likely to have heard of any accidents. My fears vanished when I heard of a message which came for Erchy requesting him to pick up the same party, intact, and return them to the mainland. The gift of prognostication was not, it seemed, to be one of my attributes. I felt no regret.

The 'Sheehan'

WE FINISHED the pot of tea and the two men were relaxed and comfortable, smoking cigarettes and indulging in desultory argument about boats and cattle with rarely an acknowledgment of my presence. Erchy smoked half of his third cigarette and then with an exclamation threw the rest of it into the fire. Hector gave him a questioning glance.

'Ach, they're after makin' my throat dry. This cold's taken a hold of me, I'm after thinkin'.'

'Let's make another pot of tea if your throat's dry,' I suggested.

'It seems as if I cannot take anythin' hot,' Erchy replied. 'What I'll take is a drink of water.'

'I know,' I said, 'I've just the very thing. Morag was making butter for me today and there's a bowl of buttermilk in the cupboard at the back of the house. That will help soothe your throat.'

Erchy stayed in his chair.

'Where is tse buttermilk? I could do wiss a drink myself,' Hector said.

'In the cupboard at the back of the house,' I repeated. He wandered outside and returned with the full bowl cupped tenderly between his large hands. He put it on the table.

'Help yourself, Erchy,' I invited. Hector emptied the remains of tea from his mug and dipped it into the buttermilk.

'Come on, Erchy,' I insisted. 'You're always saying how much you like buttermilk.'

Erchy did not move. 'No thanks,' he said awkwardly. 'I would never take a drink of buttermilk from a woman unless she was a relative.'

I looked at him in amazement. 'Why ever not?' I demanded.

'Well, I would not, then. An' nor would any man that belongs to my family.'

'But what's wrong with accepting buttermilk. Is there some superstition about it?'

'It's no superstition,' returned Erchy warmly. 'It's somethin' that happened an' it happened to my grandfather an' his brother. Since then there's not one of us would take a drink of buttermilk from a stranger.'

'I'm hardly a stranger, Erchy,' I pointed out, a little disgruntled.

But he would not be persuaded, and I noticed that though Hector had filled his mug he had not yet raised it to his lips.

'I don't know this story about buttermilk and your grandfather,' I confessed. 'But if you're not going to accept my offer you ought at least to explain why.'

Erchy settled himself back in his chair, 'Well, you know the Sheehan?' he asked.

I nodded. I had heard of the 'Sheehan' (Fairy Hill) and discovered it quite by accident one day when searching for a heronry which the locals knew existed but which was not, so far as I could discover, marked on any of the bird maps. I had floundered through bogs, waded streams, climbed in and out of corries and had at last, to my great delight, come upon indisputable evidence of a heronry. Returning via a corrie I had never previously explored I could not help noticing a raised area of greenness, roughly rectangular in shape, set amidst the sedge brown moor. In the centre of the greenness rose a small heathery knoll, about eight foot in diameter and not much higher than myself. Strewn haphazardly around the knoll were several large white stones. I was tired and the knoll amidst the greenness looked inviting, so I sat down and leaned back against the springy heather. Almost immediately I became aware that the ground was warm beneath my bottom. I sat up and patted the knoll. There was no doubt of its warmth. I got up and walked round it, assessing its situation and pondering upon the explanation, scientific or factual, for its being able to absorb, retain and exude more warmth than other knolls, for it was not the first time that day I had rested and at no time had I found the ground anything but damp and chill. Eventually I decided it must be something to do with all the rabbit burrows around the base of the knoll; possibly it enclosed such a large colony that enough heat was generated to penetrate the covering of soil and heather roots. I sat down again, letting my imagination play with a children's story that began with a warm knoll in a strange green place with

white stones. But it was no such tale for children that Erchy
related to me now.

'It was one time when my grandfather an' his brother took
the cattle to the spring sale. It was fifteen miles they had to
walk them, so when they got there they enjoyed themselves
with a bitty of the money they made. You know, takin' a
good dram. Then they bought the few things they were
needin' an' a couple of bolls of meal that they took on their
backs an 'started the journey home. It was about four o'clock
in the evenin' an' pretty warm, an' when they were about a
third the way they began wishin' they hadn't taken so much
whisky and complainin' their mouths were dry.

' "What wouldn't I give for a good drink of buttermilk to
cool my whisky down," says my grandfather's brother,
Finlay was his name.

' "Aye," says my grandfather. "But there's no chance of a
drink of any sort till we get to the next croft an' that's another
four miles yet."

'Just then they see a woman comin' towards them, carryin'
a pail an' a bowl. She's a fine lookin' woman—not young,
not old, an' she has her hair in two long pleats.

' "Well, boys," she greets them. "Am I not hearin' you
sayin' you have a fancy for a drink of buttermilk? Here then.
I just finished makin' butter myself. Take a drink an' ease
your thirst." She pours out milk from the pail into the bowl
an' holds it out to them. My grandfather gets suspicious an'
refuses, an' he wasn't pleased to see Finlay take the bowl an'
drink up the buttermilk. Then the woman says, "My house
is just in the glen there, will you not come an' rest yourselves
for a wee whiley?" Now my grandfather knows that this
woman is no ordinary woman because he went this way many
times an' he never saw a house of any sort in the glen. But
Finlay seems to suspect nothin'. "Come on," he urges, an'
follows the woman. My grandfather knows he must follow
his brother an' try to save him from the fairies before they
have complete power over him, so he follows too an' they

come to this green place with the heathery cnoc in the middle.
In this cnoc there's a dark passage leadin' to a thick heavy
door and from beyond comes the sounds of music an'
laughter an' dancin'. Finlay's all excited but my grandfather
knows it's a trap and tries to persuade him to turn away. But
the door opens an' Finlay follows the woman in. My grandfather thinks he's gone for good but then he remembers that
after the sale he bought a packet of iron nails that he has in
his pocket, so pretendin' he's tired with carryin' his boll of
meal he stumbles against the door an' drives a nail into it so
the fairies won't see it. Without that nail, he knew he would
never be able to go out through that door again. Inside
they're invited to dance an' Finlay, still with his boll of meal
on his back, joins in. My! but how they dance, those folk,
swingin' Finlay round from one to the other an' all the time
to strange wild music that made my grandfather so feared
he pulled moss to stop his ears from hearin' it.

' "If you won't join our dancin' sit yourself down on the
hearth." That was the woman with the buttermilk speakin' to
my grandfather again. She showed him the white hearth
stones, but he wouldn't sit down an' stood with his boll of
meal on his back, waitin' a chance to slip a nail into his
brother's pocket an' so help him to escape from the fairies.
But Finlay never stopped dancin' for a second an' even with
the boll of meal on his back he never sweated a drop or
showed a trace of tiredness. At last Finlay swings against his
brother, an' there's his chance. My grandfather got the nail
in his pocket an' Finlay seemed to wake from a dream. The
two of them made for the door, pulled it open an' ran out.
They didn't stop runnin' till they'd done about four miles an'
could see the next croft. There Finlay collapsed as if he was
dead an' my grandfather couldn't wake him. He went for
help to the croft house an' told them the story, an' soon all
the men of the village banded together, called on the
minister begging him to go with them, an' followed my
grandfather to the place of the green grass an' the heathery

cnoc. But they found no passage an' no door. An' though they took spades an' dug at the cnoc they found nothin' to prove my grandfather's story except for some white stones that looked like hearth stones an' these they threw out, scattering them around the cnoc.'

'An' a nail, did tsey not?' Hector reminded him. 'A shiny new nail, like as if it was never used.'

'Aye,' Erchy remembered. 'Aye, you're right.'

'It was lucky forhim he bought tsose nails,' Hector murmured.

'What about Finlay?' I asked. 'Did he recover from his ordeal?'

'He was never the same again,' replied Erchy. 'He slept for three whole days before they could wake him an' when they did wake him he had such a stammer they couldn't understand much of what he said. He never got rid of it. Never.'

I indicated Hector's mug of buttermilk, still untouched. 'So you don't trust me enough to drink my buttermilk,' I teased them.

Hector gallahtly took up the mug, wished my good health and drank deeply. He smacked his lips. 'Tsat was good,' he said.

Erchy said: 'It's all right for him. You notice he's wearin' tackety boots.'

'Oh, Erchy,' I laughed. 'Can you imagine anything less like a fairy than I am? Honestly? Wouldn't I need to be a "fine lookin' woman" if I wanted to inveigle you into my power. For goodness's sake take a good long look at me and see if you can see the slightest resemblance to a fairy.'

I am no beauty at the best of times and I knew how revolting I must look after my dose of 'flu. Lank hair, puffy red-rimmed eyes, red nose and pale cracked lips. Erchy stared at me long and hard.

'Well?' I demanded cynically. 'Anything seductive in my appearance?'

'No,' he retorted relentlessly, and picking up the bowl of buttermilk he drank it to the last drop.